Torah & Company

The weekly portion of Torah, accompanied by generous helpings of Mishnah and Gemara, served up with discussion questions to spice up your Sabbath table

Judith Z. Abrams

Ben Yehuda Press

Published by Ben Yehuda Press
430 Kensington Road
Teaneck, NJ 07666

http://www.BenYehudaPress.com

For permission to reprint, including distribution of the material in this book as part of a synagogue or school newsletter, please contact: Permissions, Ben Yehuda Press, 430 Kensington Road, Teaneck, NJ 07666. Email permissions@ BenYehudaPress.com.

Ben Yehuda Press books may be purchased for educational, business or sales promotional use. For information, please contact: Special Markets, Ben Yehuda Press, 430 Kensington Road, Teaneck, NJ 07666. Email markets@ BenYehudaPress.com.

ISBN 0-9769862-1-3

Library of Congress Control Number: 2005931730

FIRST EDITION

05 06 07 08 09   / 10 9 8 7 6 5 4 3 2 1

This book is dedicated to
Mary Rose, Debby, and Leah

Acknowledgments

I thank God for the opportunity to have done this work and I thank the many people who have helped in that process. Yori Yanover and Larry Yudelson gave me the original internet forum in which most of this book was composed.

Of course, I thank my family for their steadfast love, support and understanding.

Contents

Introduction: Why Torah & Company?

The Babylonian Talmud (Avodah Zarah 19b) teaches that we should spend a third of our lives studying Torah, a third of our lives studying Mishnah, and a third of our lives studying Gemara.

The importance of the Torah to Judaism is self-evident. Just look at the schedule of services on a Shabbat morning–or on a Monday or Thursday morning, for that matter. You will find that the Torah reading takes center stage.

But Mishnah? Gemara? How did they get into the picture? And what *are* they anyway?

The short answer is that the Mishnah is the oldest code of Jewish law. It says what to do, when to do it, and how to do it. Gemara is the broader discussion, often connecting the Mishnah to its sources in the Torah. Written down, it's the substance of the two Talmuds (the Bavli, or Babylonian, and its older, more obscure relative, the Yerushalmi, or Jerusalem (or occasionally, Palestinian) Talmud. (More details about the rabbinic texts used in this book can be found starting on page 124 of this present volume.)

Taken together, one has the Written Torah, and the two major components of the Oral Torah–in other words, a well-balanced menu.

I hear you ask: A third of our lives? Starting when? And what about my day job?

Good questions. The Talmud itself explains that since we don't know how long our lives will last, we should split each day, and our study be comprised of a third Torah, a third Mishnah and a third Gemara. And since most of us (except for the occasional lucky teacher or author) can't spend all day studying, the traditional prayer book provides representative passages from the Torah, Mishnah, and Gemara to provide us with a minimum daily dose. (You'll find these texts in the material for Naso, page 70.)

Our book expands this principle to our weekly study of the Torah. I've chosen a key passage from each week's Torah portion and selected passages from the Mishnah and the Gemara (and on occasion, Midrash) that are thematically related.

And since a key element of Torah study is oral study–the discussion–I've included questions corresponding to each passage to get you started.

A BLESSING ON YOUR TORAH STUDY

The sages of the Talmud considered Torah study both a gift from God and a commandment. And like all gifts from God, and all commandments, there is a blessing to be recited before we begin. (In fact, the sages were so enthusiastic that the blessing in the traditional prayerbook is actually an amalgalm of three separate versions.)

The blessing goes like this:

בָּרוּךְ אַתָּה יְיָ אֱלֹהֵינוּ מֶלֶךְ הָעוֹלָם אֲשֶׁר קִדְּשָׁנוּ בְּמִצְוֹתָיו וְצִוָּנוּ לַעֲסוֹק בְּדִבְרֵי תוֹרָה׃

"Blessed are You, Adonai our God, who has sanctified us with commandments and commanded us to be busy studying Torah." (Bavli Berachot 11b)

For the rabbis, reciting the blessing was an important signal -- to God, and to themselves -- that their study was not simply an intellectual pursuit, but a sacred endeavor. Curious Roman philosophers might study Torah along with the writings of other cultures, but the rabbis wanted to make clear that they, at least, were acting out their idea of fulfilling God's commands. Without the blessing, they said, you might still have the joy of study, but not the holy benefit of fulfilling the mitzvah. It's a bit like logging in your frequent flier number before you fly. If you don't register, you still get the trip but you miss the bonus of accruing the miles.

The blessing is also a reminder that, as a mitzvah, the study of Torah is in some very august company (see page 70 for details).

Gematria

One of the most enjoyable forms of Torah study is through Jewish numerology. Each Hebrew letter has a numerical value as demonstrated in the chart, below:

alef = 1	zayin =7	mem=40	kuf=100
bet= 2	chet =8	nun=50	resh=200
gimel =3	tet=9	samech=60	shin=300
dalet = 4	yod=10	ayin=70	taf=400
hey = 5	caf=20	pey=80	
vav = 6	lamed=30	tzadi=90	

Not only will we be looking at the numerical values of words, but also the numbers of words in sentences and what these numbers mean. For example, the word *chai* (*chet* (8) + *yud* (10)= life (18) is one of the most commonly known pieces of gematria in our culture today. We'll be encountering more sophisticated and fun types of numerology in our studies.

ANOTHER PERTINENT NUMERICAL POINT

The ancient Mesopotamians had a base-60 number system. Thus one-sixtieth would be the smallest whole unit in their system. We use this number system today without even thinking about it: there are 60 seconds in a minute and 60 minutes in an hour and 360 degrees in a circle. This is also why numbers that divide into 60 are so important in Judaism.

How to use this book

☞ Choose a section based on the week's Torah portion or an upcoming holiday. Generally speaking, during the week one studies the Torah portion that will be read the following Shabbat morning.

☞ The texts have no particular order other than that of the Jewish calendar, so feel free to jump in anywhere at anytime. Each week stands alone. We make no assumption that you've read the previous week's texts.

☞ Read through the texts. See what they have in common.

☞ All translations are my own. They are much more free-flowing than is my usual style. I do this expecting that this book will be used without any additional commentaries or reference volumes.

☞ Some of the texts may seem hopelessly technical. Don't be discouraged if their meaning isn't immediately obvious. You'll find explanations in the corresponding question section.

☞ After a once over, read through each text again and its corresponding discussion questions. If you're studying around the table or in a group, feel free to discuss the questions that interest you and to ignore the rest.

☞ If you want to join in the chain of Torah study, then write in some of your own thoughts where space permits.

Bereishit

BEGINNINGS

Genesis 1:1

In a beginning God created the heavens and the earth.

Mishnah Hagigah 2:1

The Work of Creation may not be taught to more than one student at a time.... Whoever contemplates these four questions, it would have been better for him not to have come into the world: What is above the world? What is below? What is before? What is after?

Bavli Eruvin 13b

For three years, there was a dispute between the School of Shammai and the School of Hillel, the former claiming: The law is in agreement with our views. And the latter claiming: The law is in agreement with our views. Then a voice came out of heaven and said: Both of these views are the words of the living God, but the law goes according to the School of Hillel's rulings. But if both are the words of the living God, why is the law set according to School of Hillel'? Because they behaved modestly and like *mensches*. They studied Shammai's rules as well as their own and even mentioned Shammai's words before they said their own.

Discussion Questions

1. The first word of the Torah, *b'reshit,* is generally translated "In *the* beginning." Strictly speaking, however, it means "In *a* beginning". How does this change your understanding of this verse?

2. Do you agree with the Mishnah's assertion that questioning the mechanics of Creation is an invasion of God's privacy? Does God have some secrets that shouldn't be explored? Do you feel entitled to your secrets? Does having secrets make you distant from your loved ones? Does keeping secrets sometimes allow you to be closer to them?

3. It appears, from this passage of the Bavli, that God speaks in many voices and that there may be many correct answers. This should lead to tolerance and humility. Do you think you could practice this intellectual discipline in your own life...thinking that God's truth is everywhere and that success goes to those who act like gentlemen?

Noah

PROCREATION

Genesis 9:6-7

(God blessed Noah after the flood, saying:)
Whoever sheds a man's blood by man shall his blood be shed: for in God's image was man made. And as for you, be fruitful and multiply: Bring forth abundant life in the earth and multiply life on it.

Mishnah Yebamot 6:6

A man shall not abstain from the performance of the duty of maintaining the human race unless he already has children. How many children? The School of Shammai ruled: two males. The School of Hillel ruled: a male and a female. For it is stated in Bible, "Male and female created He them. (Genesis 1:28)"

Sifra on Leviticus 19:18

"Love your neighbor as yourself" (Leviticus 19:18). Rabbi Akiba said: This is the greatest principle in the Torah. Ben Azzai quoted the verse, "This is the book of the generations of Adam. In that day, God created human beings in the likeness of God did God make him" (Genesis 5:1). He said: This is a principle greater than that.

Discussion Questions

1. This Torah passage is an example of "Jewish karma," that is, the concept *middah k'neged middah*, literally, "measure for measure," or more colloquially, "what goes around comes around." Have you seen evidence of this in your own life? Can you think of other biblical examples of this concept?

2. In rabbinic literature, students are considered as if they are the children of their teachers. Using this reckoning, how many children do you have? How could you acquire more? How do you "parent" those who learn from you?

3. If you do not love yourself and you treat your neighbor the way you treat yourself, you might treat your neighbor quite badly. How does reminding yourself that everyone is created in God's image insure that you'll treat others better? Will you treat yourself better because of this teaching?

Lech L'cha

UNDERTAKINGS

Genesis 12:1

(Terach, the father of Avram–later known as Abraham–has just died in Haran.)
And the Lord said to Avram, Get you out (*lech l'cha*) of your country, and from your kindred, and from your father's house, to the land that I will show you.

Mishnah Pirkei Avot 5:4

Abraham, our father, was tested ten times and he withstood all ten tests to let everyone know how great was his love for God.

Bavli Baba Batra 163a

How much space should be between two lines of writing? Rav Yitzhak ben Elazar said: As much, for example, as is required for the writing of *lech l'cha* (Genesis 12:1 and Genesis 22:2) one above the other.

*A section of Genesis 22,
with the words* lech l'cha *highlighted.*

Discussion Questions

1. The Hebrew of the Torah verse lends itself to many midrashic possibilities. Translated literally, *lech l'cha* can mean to "go to yourself." Can one "go to oneself" (become oneself) by attending to God's communiqués, and beginning an outward journey? Or would an inward journey be more in order? Abraham is the only person in the entire Tanach to be commanded with the words *lech l'cha*. Why do you think that is?

2. The ten trials of Abraham are listed in Avot d'Rabbi Natan 33 (the earliest commentary on Pirkei Avot). They are as follows: two trials when he left Haran, two with his two sons, two with his two wives, one in the war of the Kings (Genesis 21:22-34), one at the "covenant of the pieces" (Genesis 15), one when he was thrown into a furnace by Nimrod and one at the circumcision. These are grouped, in Avot, with the ten utterances that created the world, the ten generations from Adam to Noah, and the ten generations from Noah to Abraham, the ten wonders God performed in Egypt, and the ten things created on the eve of Shabbat. What do these lists of "ten" have in common? Is there any list of "ten" you'd want to add from our own era?

3. The Gemara here is discussing how much space there needs to be between lines of text in a document. Note the illustration on the facing page. The Hebrew letter *lamed* extends the furthest upward and the letter *chaf sofit* extends the furthest downward. Therefore, the scribe would have to leave enough room to accomodate the possibility of *lech l'cha* appearing on two lines, one directly above the other.

What do you make of the symbolism of these letters: That *lech l'cha* extends in the furthest directions up and down? That *lech l'cha* in numerology is 100, i.e., 10 x 10?

What do you make of the fact that the second usage of *lech l'cha*, in chapter 22, is part of Abraham's 10th trial, the command to offer Isaac on the altar?

Vayeira

SENSITIVITY

Genesis 18:12-13

(God promised Sarah, 90, that she would have a child.)
Therefore, Sarah laughed sadly within herself, saying: "Is there any chance, given how old I am and how old how old my husband is, that I could have a child?" And the Lord said to Abraham: Why did Sarah laugh, saying: "How could I, who am so old, give birth?"

Mishnah Baba Metzia 4:10

Just as harm can be done in buying and selling, so harm can be done with words.

So one must not ask a seller: "What is the price of this article?" if he has no intention of buying it.

Nor should one say to a repentant sinner: "Remember your former deeds."

Nor should one say to a son of converts: "Remember the deeds of your ancestors, because it is written, 'You shall neither wrong nor oppress a stranger (convert)(Exodus 22:20)'."

Bavli Shabbat 23b

If one has only enough money to buy oil for either the house light for Shabbat, or the Hanukkah light, but not both, the former is preferable on account of the peace of his home.

If one has only enough money to buy either the house light or wine for the Sanctification of the Day (*Kiddush*) but not both, the house light is preferable on account of the peace of his home.

Discussion Questions

1. Note the difference between what Sarah says and what God tell Abraham she says. The most frequently cited explanation for God's change of Sarah's words is the desire to foster *shlom bayit*, "household peace" between husband and wife. Can you think of other reasons God might have altered Sarah's words in the fashion reported in the Torah?

2. This mishnah shows the importance of feelings in Judaism. Hurting someone with words is equated to monetary crimes. It helps to know that the word ger, "stranger", can also mean "convert." What does the inconvenienced sales clerk have in common with the repentant sinner and the convert?

3. The Gemara demonstrates the relative value of different ritual acts based on the needs of *shalom beito,* i.e., household peace. Do you ever experience discord because of religious choices? Given that household harmony is given such a high priority, how might you solve those problems?

Chayei Sarah

MOURNING

Genesis 23:2

And Sarah died in Kiryat-Arba, that is Hebron, in the land of Canaan and Abraham came to mourn for Sarah and to weep for her.

Mishnah Moed Katan 3:8-9

When a funeral is held during the middle days of Passover and Sukkot, women may wail for the dead but they do not clap their hands. But Rabbi Yishmael says: Those who are close to the corpse may clap their hands....

What is a wail? When all the women sing together.

What is a dirge? When one woman sings and the rest answer after her.

Bavli Moed Katan 28a

Why is the story of Miriam's death (Numbers 20:1) placed next to the chapter concerning the red heifer (Numbers 19)? It is there to tell you that just as the red heifer atones for sin,* so does the death of the righteous atone for sin.

---

*See Parah, p. 78, for more details about the red heifer ritual.

Discussion Questions

1. In the Torah scroll, the word which describes Abraham's crying, "*v'livkotah*," has a small, half-sized Hebrew letter *kaf* in it:

One commentator suggests that this is because he only cried a bit, since she had reached the good old age of 127. Are there some deaths which call forth fewer tears than others?

2. This text outlines the way women coordinated and led the mourning at funerals. What do you think of the Mishnah taking it for granted that women are not only singing in public but are also leading the funeral ritual? What do you think of the manner in which the ritual is conducted?

3. The passage in Numbers describes how the ashes of the red heifer are used to purify people from the impurity contracted through contact with a corpse. What do you think is meant in this Gemara when it says that the deaths of righteous persons offer atonement for the living? How does the "blanket" atonement afforded by the righteous, or the red heifer, affect personal accountability for our own actions?

Toldot

VISION

Genesis 27:1

(Isaac prepares to bless his eldest son, Esau.)
And it came to pass that Isaac was old and his eyes were dim and he was
prevented from seeing.

Mishnah Negaim 2:3

A priest blind in one eye or whose sight is dim may not inspect the
symptoms of scale disease, as it is said regarding the process of inspection,
"as far as appears to the priest" (Leviticus 13:12).

Sifra Kedoshim 3:13-14

"And before a blind person do not place a stumbling block." This means
blind in a certain matter, i.e., someone who has a "blind spot". If a man
asks you if the daughter of So-and-so is eligible to marry a priest, do not
say to him, "she's fit," when she is unfit.... This matter of giving honest
advice is a matter of the heart, as it is said, "And you shall fear the Lord
your God, I am the Lord" (Leviticus 19:14). Only God knows whether
you were sincere or not.

Discussion Questions

1. This information about Isaac's vision directly precedes the passage wherein Jacob obtains Esau's blessing from their father. The implication is that Jacob might not have fooled Isaac had he been fully sighted. Was Isaac indeed fooled? Did Jacob steal the blessing or did Isaac see through the ruse all along?

2. Sight was intrinsic to the priest's ability to perform the task of correctly diagnosing scale disease. It was so important that priests were not allowed to function in this role if even one of their eyes was impaired. What kinds of jobs today require some special physical attribute (e.g., perfect eyesight for pilots or astronauts or being over 5'10" and weighing under 120 pounds for runway models)? How does it feel if you make the cut? How does it feel if you don't?

3. Sight is often metaphorically extended to refer to insight, as it is in this passage from the midrash. Do you know your own blind spots? How do they make you vulnerable? How might you improve your "vision"?

Vayeitzei

HEAVEN'S GATE

Genesis 28:16-17

(Jacob, on his way to find a wife, stops and has a dream about angels and ladders.)
And Jacob woke out of his sleep and he said: Surely God is in this place and I didn't know it! And he was afraid and said: How awe-full is this place! This is none other than the house of God and this is the gate of heaven.

Mishnah. Megillah 4:4

The one that reads in the Torah may not read less than three verses, and he does not read more than one verse at a time to the translator*. But when he reads from the Prophets (e.g., Haftara), he may read three verses at a time.

Bavli Tamid 32a

Alexander of Macedon said to the sages: Who is called wise?

They said: The one who can see the future.

He said to them: Who is called a mighty man?

They said: The one who conquers his appetites.

He said to them: Who is a called a rich man?

They said: The one who is happy with what he has.

---

* *In the time of the Mishnah, the Torah reading was accompanied by a line-by-line translation from the biblical Hebrew into Aramaic, the vernacular.*

Discussion Questions

1. Could you be at the gateway to heaven and not know it? How *would* you know it? Is the gateway on the Temple Mount in Jerusalem (the traditional interpretation of where Jacob's dream took place), or might the gate open anywhere?

2. How does reading three verses of Torah turn a place into a gateway to heaven or into a kind of Mount Sinai?

3. In the ultimate holy place, and/or when you reach a certain level of mystic understanding, straightforward logic no longer applies. The sages here are demonstrating this higher reality in their answers to Alexander the Great. How does the sages' mystical reality reflect good, common-sense advice? In other words, can leading a spiritually enlightened life help one to function better in the "real world"?

Vayishlach

Genesis 32:10-11

(On the eve of his reunion with brother Esau, Jacob is afraid.)

And Jacob said: God of my father Abraham and God of my father Isaac, the Lord who did say to me: Return to your country and to your land, the land where you were born, and I will make sure things go well for you. I am scarcely worth all the love and all the truth that you have done for me, Your servant.

Mishnah Berachot 4:3-4

Rabban Gamaliel says: Every day a person should pray the Eighteen Benedictions. Rabbi Joshua says: They can pray an abbreviated form of the Eighteen Benedictions. Rabbi Akiba says: If he knows it fluently, let him pray the full Eighteen Benedictions, but if not, let him pray an abbreviated form of the Eighteen Benedictions. Rabbi Eliezer says: If a man prays regularly but with no feeling then he is not really asking God for anything in his prayer.

Bavli Berachot 3a

Rabbi Jose said: One time I was walking on the road, and I entered one of the ruins in Jerusalem to pray. Elijah (may his memory be a blessing!) came and waited for me at the door till I finished my prayer. After I finished my prayer, he spoke with me.

Elijah said: "Peace be with you, my rabbi!"

I said to him: "Peace be with you my rabbi and my teacher!"

Elijah said: "My son, why did you go into this ruin?"

I said: "To pray."

Elijah said: "You should have prayed on the road."

I said to him: "I was afraid that passers-by might interrupt me."

Elijah said: "You ought to have said a shortened prayer."

In that one moment, concluded Rabbi Jose, I learned from him three things: I learned that one does not enter a ruin, one may pray on the road, and one who prays on the road prays a short prayer.

Discussion Questions

1. Jacob utters this prayer when he is returning home after many years, still desperately afraid of his brother Esau and the ill will caused by his theft of the birthright. Jacob prays, calling upon the God of his *"father"* Abraham and his actual father, Isaac. In what way can a person function as your parent, sibling, cousin, etc. even when he or she is not legally entitled to that role? How is Abraham more a father to Jacob than Isaac?

2. The "Eighteen Benediction" (*Shmoneh Esrei*) are the prayers known collectively as the weekday *Amidah,* or "standing" prayer. Look at the flexibility with regards to prayer expressed in this mishnah. Tease out the differences between the views of Rabban Gamliel, Rabbi Joshua, and Rabbi Akiba. Who is stricter? Who is more lenient? What do you make of Rabbi Eliezer's rule about intention?

3. Have you ever found a place that was especially conducive to prayer? What made it so? Does your physical environment have an effect on your prayer?

Vayeishev

DREAMS

Genesis 37:5-6

(Joseph is a seventeen-year-old shepherd, who is his father's favorite son.)
And Joseph dreamed a dream and he told his brothers about it and they hated him even more. And he said to them: Listen, now, to this dream which I dreamed.

Mishnah Pirkei Avot 3:15

Everything is foreseen but free will is given. And the world is judged with goodness and everything depends on the abundance of good deeds.

Bavli Berachot 57b

Five things are a sixtieth part of something else: fire, honey, Shabbat, sleep, and dreams.

Fire is 1/60th of Hell.

Honey is 1/60th of manna.

Shabbat is 1/60th of the world to come.

Sleep is 1/60th of death.

A dream is 1/60th of prophecy.

Discussion Questions

1. Why do Joseph's brothers hate him? Because he dreams? Because in his dreams, Joseph wields power over his brothers? Is it because Jacob loves him best? Or is it something else?

2. Could the story have had a different outcome? Could Joseph's brothers have intervened earlier and simply said, "Stop telling us the dreams!"? Could Joseph have been less self-absorbed and noticed the effect of his dreams on his brothers? Where is free will evident in this story?

3. The Gemara hints* that so many of the treasures of our world are hidden; that we experience only the tip of the iceberg of God's reality. What else can you think of that fits into the formula: X is 1/60th of Y?

---

* *Refer back to page viii for a discussion of the significance of the number 60 in the ancient world.*

Mikeitz

THE WORLD TO COME

Genesis 42:38

(Jacob wishes to keep his youngest son back, when the brothers return to Egypt for food.)
And Jacob said: "My son Benjamin shall not go down with you for his brother is dead and he alone is left of his mother's children. If something unexpected should happen to him on the way, you would bring down my gray hairs with sorrow to the afterlife."

Mishnah Sanhedrin 10:1

All Israel has a portion in the world to come.... These are they who have no portion in the world to come: the one that says that resurrection of the dead is not from the Torah.

Bavli Shabbat 31a

When one is led in for judgment after death one will be asked:

Were you honest in business?
Did you fix times for learning?
Did you engage in procreation?
Did you hope for salvation?
Did you engage in dialectics of wisdom?
Did you understand one thing from another?

Discussion Questions

1. Jacob says he will go down to the afterlife in sorrow. What do you imagine this afterlife would be like?

2. The Mishnah here clearly affirms that there is an afterlife in Judaism. Not only that, the Mishnah teaches that the dead will be resurrected in this afterlife. What are your ideas about resurrection? About reincarnation?

3. How are you scoring so far with these questions? (Students are considered equivalent to children, so be sure to include that in your scoring.)

Does it help to know "the questions on the test" ahead of time?

Are you surprised by the first question? Are you surprised that there is no such question as, "Did you light Shabbat candles?"

Vayigash

KNOW BEFORE WHOM YOU STAND

Genesis 47:7-10

(Jacob's family has been reunited with Joseph in Egypt.)
And Joseph brought Jacob, his father, and stood him before Pharaoh, and Jacob blessed Pharaoh. And Pharaoh said to Jacob: How old are you? And Jacob said to Pharaoh: I have wandered for 130 years; few and evil have been the length of my days. I have not approached the number of years that my fathers lived in their wanderings. And Jacob blessed Pharaoh and left Pharaoh's presence.

Mishnah Berachot 9:4

One who enters a city should pray twice: Once when entering it and once when leaving it. Ben Azzai says: Four times: twice when entering it and twice when leaving it. And one should give thanks for what has passed and cry out to God for what is to come in the future.

Bavli Berachot 28b

When Rabbi Eliezer fell fatally ill, his students went to visit him.

His students said to him: "Our Rabbi, teach us how to live so that we might merit the world to come."

Rabbi Eliezer said to them: "Be sure to honor your colleagues...and set your children between the knees of the students of the sages. When you pray, know before Whom you are standing. By doing these things you will merit a place in the world to come."

Discussion Questions

1. Is Jacob's "blessing" truly a blessing or is it simply a greeting? How does a shepherd have the nerve to bless Pharaoh? How might Jacob have blessed Pharaoh on entering? On leaving? Why does Jacob speak so bitterly before Pharaoh? Are they competing with each other for Joseph's time and love? If so, who wins?

2. The mishnah suggests a spiritual discipline: Pray prospectively, and thank retrospectively; "Please," and "Thank you," as it were. In practice, one would pray on approach to the city, and then thank God upon actually entering its gates, and so forth. Can you think of other ways to use this pattern in your relationship with God? With others?

3. Rabbi Eliezer was excommunicated for stubbornly refusing to concede defeat when he was outvoted by all his colleagues. They came to visit him only on his deathbed. Given that context, what do you make of his admonitions to his students?

Vayechi

PROMISES

Genesis 50:25-26

(After a full life, Joseph addresses his brothers, with whom he has made peace.)
And Joseph made the Israelites take this oath: God will surely remember that you have promised to take my bones out of Egypt. And when Joseph was 110 years old he died and they embalmed him and put him in a coffin in Egypt.

Mishnah Pirkei Avot 4:18

Rabbi Shimon ben Elazar said: Do not try to appease your friend when he is angry. Do not try to console him when his dead lie before him. Do not question him when he makes a vow. And do not try to see him when he is in disgrace.

Bavli Ketubot 111a

"And Joseph made the Israelites take this oath...you shall take my bones away from here." Rabbi Hanina said: Here is this verse's inner meaning. Joseph knew he was a completely righteous man and that even if he died outside the land of Israel he would live in the world to come. So why did he burden his brothers by making them vow to make sure they would take his bones back to the land of Israel, a trip of four hundred Persian miles? Because he was worried that he might be found unworthy to roll through the cavities that would be used by others who were resurrected and then brought to the land of Israel.

Discussion Questions

1. Why do you think the book of Genesis closes with these words? How do they form a link to the book of Exodus and the entire saga of the Israelites in Egypt?

2. What do all of Rabbi Shimon ben Elazar's guidelines have in common? How are they a reflection of sound principles of human interaction? Would you add any "rules of discretion" to this list? Why is this teaching especially important in these days of instant communication via email, for example?

3. According to the sages, when the messiah comes, the dead will be resurrected and then will roll through underground tunnels to the Land of Israel. Therefore, the sages wonder why Joseph made his brothers promise to bring him to the Land of Israel. Joseph did not want to assume that he would be considered righteous enough to roll through these tunnels. How do you imagine resurrected people making their way to the Land of Israel? How do you envision the resurrection? (The sages thought that the souls would be freeze-dried and then a special dew would fall and revive them.) What burdens do we put on our descendants because of our self-doubts?

Chazak, chazak, v'nitchazek

Be strong, strong, and be strengthened!

Hadaran alach! Hadaran alach!

We shall return to you, Mishnah! We shall return to you, Gemara!

When we finish reading a book of the Torah, we affirm how much strength it gives us by reciting the first sentence, above.

When we complete a book of Mishnah or Gemara, we vow in Aramaic to return to that book. (We don't have to promise to return to a book of the Torah because we know we will read it again next year.)

Shmot

GOD'S NAME

Exodus 3:13-14

(Moses receiving his charge at the Burning Bush.)
And Moses said to God: Look, when I come to the Israelites and say
to them, the God of your fathers has sent me to you. They'll say to me:
What is His name? Then what shall I say to them?

And God said to Moses: Tell the Israelites that *Eheyeh asher eheyeh* ("I
am that I am") sent you to them.

Mishnah Berachot 2:1

If one were reading the passage of the *Shema* in the Torah (Deuteronomy
6:4: "Hear O Israel...") and the time for reciting the Shema arrived, if he
had intended to recite the *Shema* he has fulfilled his obligation, and if
not, then he has not fulfilled his obligation.

Bavli Baba Batra 73a

The wave that sinks a ship appears with a white fringe of fire at its crest,
and it subsides when stricken with clubs upon which are engraved, "I am
that I am, Yah, the Lord of Hosts, Amen, Amen, Selah."

Discussion Questions

1. God's name, mentioned here, is translated in many, many ways. Various different translations I have seen are: "I-am-that-I-am"; or "I-will-be-what-I-will-be"; or "I-will-become-what-I-will-be". What do you think this name of God means?

This name of God is associated with healing in Judaism. Why do you think that might be?

2. In making use of God's name, what roles do intention and belief play? Even if one is outwardly performing the mitzvah of reciting the *Shema,* the act is invalid without intention. What crosses your mind when you say (or hear) the *Shema*?

3. Imagine the sailors' behavior as a metaphor. Could you conceive a misfortune "trying to sink your ship" which could be beaten back by reciting God's names over and over, like mantras? Why do you think these names were used and not some others?

Va'eira

POWER

Exodus 7:19

(The first plague)
And the Lord said to Moses: Say to Aaron: Take your rod and stretch out your hand upon the waters of Egypt, upon their streams, upon their canals, upon their ponds and upon all their pools of water so that they will become blood. And the waters became blood throughout all the land of Egypt, even water collected in wood and stone vessels.

Mishnah Rosh Hashanah 3:8

"And when Moses held up his hand, holding the rod of God, Israel prevailed in its battle against Amalek" (Exodus 17:11). But could Moses' hands win or lose a war? Rather, this phrase teaches you that every time the Israelites looked toward heaven and dedicated their hearts to serve their Father in heaven, they would prevail, and if they did not do so, they would fall.

Bavli Megillah 31a

Every place in the Bible where you find the power of the Holy One, blessed be He mentioned, you also find His humility mentioned. This is written in the Torah, repeated in the Prophets and stated a third time in the Writings.

It is written in Torah, "For the Lord your God, He is the God of gods and the Lord of lords" (Deuteronomy 10:17); and it says immediately afterward, "He executes justice for the orphan and the widow."

It is repeated in Prophets, "For thus says the High and Lofty One, who lives on high and whose name is Holy" (Isaiah 57:15); and it says immediately afterwards, "I dwell with him that is contrite and whose spirit has fallen."

It is stated a third time, in Writings, as it is written, "Sing to the Unique One who rides upon the clouds" (Psalm 68:5); and the next verse says, "God is a father to the fatherless and a judge for the widows."

Discussion Questions

1. How do you understand the Torah text? Do you think the water actually turned to blood? Do you think heavy rains at the source of the Nile caused the water to be muddy? Does it matter?

2. Where does the power to work miracles really reside? How about the power to win battles? Are they the same?

3. What do the attributes of God's power and God's humility have in common? What does this reveal about Divine power? What do you make of the idea that God's power and mercy are mentioned together, not just in one place, but throughout the Bible?

Bo

AND YOU SHALL TEACH YOUR CHILDREN

Exodus 13:14

(Upon Leaving Egypt, before crossing the Red Sea.)
When your son shall come to you, saying: "What is this?" You shall say to him, "With a strong hand God brought us out of Egypt, from the house of slavery."

Mishnah Pesachim 10:4

They poured him a second cup of wine at the seder. And here, the son asks his father the Four Questions (and if he does not know what to say, his father teaches him what to ask).

Why is this night different from all other nights? On all other nights we eat leaven and matzah, but tonight it is all matzah? On all other nights we eat all kinds of vegetables, but tonight we eat bitter herbs? On all other nights we eat meat roasted, cooked, and boiled, but tonight we eat only roasted meat? On all other nights we don't dip even one time, and tonight we dip twice?

And according to what his son can understand, his father teaches him.

Mekhilta on Exodus 13:14, Piskha 18

The Torah refers to four children: one wise, one ignorant, one evil, and one who does not know how to ask. What does the wise son say? He says, "What are these testimonies, statutes, and judgments which the Lord our God has commanded you?" (Deuteronomy 6:20).

So you begin to explain to him the laws of Passover and continue telling him these laws until you have explained that the group that has eaten the seder together does not disband until after eating an *afikoman* dessert consisting of a piece of the Passover offering....

What does the ignorant son say? He says, "What is this?"

And you say to him, "With an outstretched hand God brought us out of Egypt, from the house of slavery" (Exodus 13:14).

Discussion Questions

1. In Hebrew, the word for "Egypt" is *Mitzrayim*, which comes from the root *tzar*, meaning, "narrow place". Have you ever had a personal escape from a narrow place? Did God's hand play a role in the experience? What happened?

2. The mishnah's question about meat refers to the Passover offering. The Mishnah has an idealistic view of reality, and does not recognize that the Temple service is no longer being practiced. By contrast, the Passover *haggadah* omits this question and reflects the Passover rituals in a post-Temple world. Which vision do you prefer?

Can you think of questions you might ask in a retelling of your journey out of your own personal Egypt?

3. Who are the four sons today? Can you see each son as the embodiment of a distinct stage of human development (Toddler=can't ask; Simple = young child; Wicked = adolescent; Wise = adult)? If so... what would it mean to teach your child at each of these distinct stages of development?

Do you find that when you yourself reach a new stage in your life, you learn things over again, as if for the first time? Or do you simply add a new perspective to what you already know?

Beshalach

SONGS

Exodus 15:11

(At the parting of the Red Sea.)
Who is like you among the gods, Lord? Who is like You, majestic among the holy ones, awesome in praises, doing wonders?

Mishnah Pirkei Avot 6:11

Everything that the Holy One Blessed be He created in His world, He created for his glory, as it is said,..."God will rule forever and ever" (Exodus 15:18).

Bavli Rosh Hashanah 31a

At the afternoon sacrifice of Shabbat, what did the Levites sing as the song accompanying the sacrifice? "Then Moses and the Israelites sang this song to the Lord saying..." (Exodus 15:1-10), and "Who is like you among the gods, Lord?" (Exodus 15:11-19), and "Then sang Israel this song, 'Spring up, Well' " (Numbers 21:17-20).

Discussion Questions

1. This verse seems to imply that the Israelites acknowledged the existence of many gods, among which God was the most powerful. Can you find some other way of interpreting this verse?

2. This is the very last mishnah in tractate *Pirkei Avot* and, as you can see, Exodus 15:18 is an important part of this mishnah. You may also have heard it in the Torah service and in other places during services. What does it mean to you that God will rule? What images does that invoke?

3. The Levites in the Temple used to sing the *Song at the Sea* (Exodus 15), and the *Song of the Well**, as the musical accompaniment to the afternoon sacrifices. These two songs are the only places the whole Bible that make use of the phrase: *az yashir*, "then sang". What do these songs have in common? Can you see a connection to Shabbat afternoon?

---

* *The* Song of the Well *reads as follows: Then Israel sang this song. Spring up well and say to it: The well dug by princes that the cream of society dug with scepters, with their staves (Numbers 21:17-18).*

Yitro

REVELATION

Exodus 20:2-3

(The Ten Commandments)
I am the Lord your God who took you out of the land of Egypt, from the house of slavery. You shall have no other Gods beside me.

Mishnah Tamid 5:1

The prayer leader in the Temple said to them: Make one benediction! And they recited the *Barechu,* and then they read the Ten Commandments, and the *Shema.*

Bavli Shabbat 88b

When Moses went up to Heaven to receive the Torah, the angels protested, arguing that the Torah should remain in their realm.

In response, Moses said: Master of the Universe! The Torah which You have given me, what is written in it?

"I am the Lord your God who took you out of the land of Egypt, from the house of slavery" (Exodus 20:2).

Said Moses to the angels: Did you go down to Egypt? Were you slaves to Pharaoh? Why then should the Torah be yours?

Discussion Questions

1. Why do you think God chose this identity to introduce the revelation at Sinai? What does it mean?

2. In the Temple, the Ten Commandments were recited along with the *Shema* and other prayers. How would you feel about including the Ten Commandments in your prayers today? Why do you think this practice was dropped?

3. There is a large body of literature, spanning many centuries, which recounts the angels' opposition to the idea of humanity receiving the Torah. Have we proven that we were worthy of the gift? Are we worthy now? Would Torah have been better off with the angels than with us?

How does our having been slaves qualify us to receive Torah?

Mishpatim

KASHRUT

Exodus 23:19

You shall not cook a kid in its mother's milk.

Mishnah Hullin 8:4

It is prohibited to cook the flesh of a clean beast in the milk of a clean beast together....* The Torah says, "in its mother's milk," which excludes a bird from the prohibition because it has no "mother's milk."

Bavli Hullin 115b

The Torah states three times, "You shall not cook a kid in its mother's milk," to teach three laws: one prohibits eating it, one prohibits deriving benefit from it, and one prohibits cooking it.

---

* Unclean animals, such as pigs, are prohibited in their own right. There is no extra prohibition of adding, for instance, cheese to a ham sandwich.

Discussion Questions

1. Some scholars suggest that this prohibition rests on the idea that mixing life and death (the mother's milk and the dead kid) is anathema to Judaism; that the whole idea of the Temple service and, by extension Israelite life, is to steer away from the taint of death. How do you keep the taint of death out of your life? What rituals do you use to accomplish this, e.g., washing your hands, wearing your seatbelt, taking vitamins, saying blessings every day that affirm your awareness of living?

2. To extend the metaphor, should we prohibit eating chickens with eggs? What else might come under such an extension?

3. What alternative meanings could you give to the Torah's three repetitions of this command?

What is your relationship to keeping kosher? What role does food play in your relationship to God and Judaism? What role does it play in your life?

Terumah

MYSTERIES

Exodus 25:11

The ark is to be covered with pure gold on the outside and inside.

Mishnah Shekalim 6:2

One time one of the priests was working in the Temple compound
and saw that one bit of the floor was different from all those around it.
He went to go tell another priest about it, but before he could finish
speaking, he died. From then on, they knew that the ark was hidden in
that spot.

Bavli Kiddushin 71a

The forty-two lettered Name is entrusted only to one who is pious, meek,
middle-aged, free from bad temper, sober, and not insistent on his rights.
And he who knows it, and carefully guards it, and observes its purity,
is beloved above and popular below, feared by man, and inherits two
worlds, this world, and the future world.

Discussion Questions

1. Why should the ark be covered in gold, both inside and out, when it is destined to be hidden from everyone's sight?

Do lavish ritual items help you concentrate on spiritual matters? If so, how? If not, why not?

2. Is it strange that during the era of the Second Temple, even the priests didn't know where the ark of the covenant was hidden? Why do you think it was so dangerous to come into contact with the ark?

3. Another form of God's presence, a forty-two letter name by which one can do magic, is also powerful and access to it is strictly limited. Why would these traits qualify a person to use this name? What attributes do you look for in a friend before you will entrust your secrets to him/her? How close are you to achieving the attributes needed to know the forty-two letter name?

Tetzaveh

A SIGN UPON YOUR HEAD

Exodus 28:36, 38

(Describing the High Priest's clothing)
And you shall make a plate of pure gold and engrave on it, like the engraving on a seal, "Holy for God" (*kodesh l'Adonai*).... And it shall be upon Aaron's forehead and Aaron shall bear the sins of the holy things which the Israelites sanctify in all their holy gifts, and it shall always be on his forehead that they may be accepted before God.

Mishnah Megillah 4:8

To make one's head-*tefillin* round, is dangerous and does not fulfill the commandment. To put *tefillin* low on the forehead, or on the palm of the hand, is the manner of heresy. To overlay them with gold, or to put the hand *tefillin* on the sleeve of one's undergarment, is the manner of outsiders.

Bavli Sukkah 46a

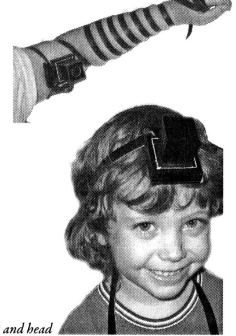

Rav Papi recited the benediction whenever he put on his *tefillin*. The rabbis of the school of Rav Ashi recited the benediction whenever they touched their *tefillin*.

Tefillin *bound on the hand (top) and head*

Discussion Questions

1. The High Priest was deemed responsible for any sins committed with the consecrated offerings that were brought to the Temple. The headpiece was meant to help him focus his thoughts and remind him of his sacred responsibility. Have you ever used a physical item to remind you of an important commitment (e.g., a wedding ring)? What significance did the item come to have?

How would you feel if you had a gold plate on your forehead proclaiming you to be consecrated to the Lord? Would it remind you to behave your best?

2. This mishnah legislates that there is only one way to correctly wear *tefillin* (the square leather boxes, containing passages of Torah, traditionally strapped on the head and arm). Do you think that people actually had round or gold *tefillin*? If so, what might they have symbolized? Could they have been associated with different groups?

If we had different sorts of *tefillin* today, what might you imagine different groups of Jews wearing?

How do you feel about wearing *tefillin*? In mishnaic times, they were worn all day long. How do you feel about outward signs of your Judaism (head coverings, *chai* necklaces)? Would you like to wear *tefillin* all day? What's the significance of the *tefillin* being square and black?

3. Do you kiss prayer books, Torah scrolls, *tefillin* or *mezuzot*? Have you seen others do so? What do you think of the practice? Does it make more sense to kiss these things once a day, or every time one has the chance?

Ki Tissa

LOOSE LIPS

Exodus 32:22-24

(Moses smashes the Tablets of the Law upon seeing the golden calf – then confronts Aaron, whom he had left in charge.)

And Aaron said: "Please don't be so angry! You know the people are bent on mischief. They said to me, 'Make us gods, which shall go before us. As for this Moses, the man that brought us up out of the land of Egypt, we don't know what has become of him.'

And I said to them: 'Who has any gold?'

Then they broke it off and gave it to me. Then I threw the gold into the fire and out came this calf."

Mishnah Megillah 4:10

The first account of the incident of the golden calf (Exodus 32:1-20) is both read and translated, the second (Exodus 32:21-25) is read but not translated.

Bavli Megillah 25b

The second account of the Calf is read but not translated. What is the second account of the Calf? From "And Moses said," up to "and Moses saw" (Exodus 32:21-25). Rabbi Shimon ben Elazar said: A person should always be careful in wording his answers, for because of the way Aaron answered Moses, the unbelievers were able to deny God, as it says, "And I threw the gold into the fire and out came this calf."

Discussion Questions

1. In the actual story of the golden calf, Aaron seems to be a much more willing participant than he does in this, his own telling. Aaron's account is tailored to suit his audience (i.e., Moses). Why do we sometimes do things we know we shouldn't? How do we rationalize our actions? How do we make amends?

2. The Mishnah is so uncomfortable with Aaron's account of the golden calf that it opposes public translation of this section. Are there some things in our pasts that are so shameful that they shouldn't be discussed? What are the arguments for, and against, a policy of silence regarding past sins?

3. The Gemara affirms the Mishnah's discomfort. The objection to Aaron's narrative is that it makes it seem as if the calf had the power to form itself. Has there ever been a time when the way you phrased an answer made all the difference in the world? What happened?

Vayakheil
GIFTING

Exodus 35:4-5, 22
(Preparing the Tabernacle)

And Moses spoke to the entire congregation of the Israelites, saying: This is the thing which the Lord commanded saying: Take from among you an offering to the Lord: whoever has a willing heart, let him bring an offering of the Lord... And they came, both men and women *(ha'anashim al hanashim*, see *Tanchuma* text below*)*, all those who had a willing heart. And they brought broaches, earrings, rings, necklaces, and all kinds of gold things.

Mishnah Yoma 3:10

Queen Helena...made a candelabra of gold over the entrance of the Sanctuary and she also made a tablet of gold with the *sotah** portion on it. (Numbers 5:11-31)

Tanhuma Ki Tissa 19

"Ha'anashim al hanashim" which literally means "the men *on* the women," teaches that the women went there first, and when the men came, they found the women had already brought their gifts. And this is a great credit to women because they had not wanted to give their jewelry to make the golden calf, for it is written, "And Aaron said to them: Break off the gold earrings which are in the ears of your wives, of your sons and of your daughters and bring them to me. And the whole group broke off the gold earrings which were in their ears and brought them to Aaron" (Exodus 32:2-3). And it doesn't say, "that were in the ears of their wives," for the women did not want to give their earrings to make the golden calf.

---

*   Sotah *is a woman suspected of adultery by her husband. Such a woman would go with her husband to the Temple to prove her innocence in a trial by ordeal. The priest would copy this section of the Torah as part of the preparation of the bitter waters which she then drank. Queen Helena's thoughtful gift assured that no couple in this delicate situation would have to wait for a scroll to be procured before they could begin the ceremony.*

Discussion Questions

1. The Torah emphasizes that giving must be done with a willing heart. The motivation with which you give charity is important. How do you use giving to mark and consecrate both the good and the bad that happens in your life?

How does this reflect the insight that your money (and, indeed, your life) does not really belong to you?

2. Queen Helena was a fabulously wealthy woman who converted to Judaism. She dedicated a gold menorah to the Temple that was positioned so that it would reflect the first light of sunrise, and sparkle over all Jerusalem, to let everyone know the precise moment to begin reciting the *Shema* had come. Likewise, she donated a plaque inscribed with the *sotah* portion so that the procedure could be performed quickly for those whose marriages were in trouble. How are these two gifts alike? How are they different? What do they reflect about Queen Helena?

3. Why do you think the women were not swept up into the "golden calf fever?" (As it turns out, they effectively saved their resources for the Tabernacle.)

Pekudei

GOD'S PRESENCE

Exodus 40:37-38

(The work on the Tabernacle is done, and the Glory of God enters the tent of meeting.)
If the cloud (above the Tabernacle that led the Israelites through the
wilderness) was not lifted, they did not travel. And they did not travel
until it was lifted. For God's cloud stayed over the Tabernacle by day.
Aand by night there was fire over the Tabernacle, so that all the Israelites
could see it in all their traveling.

Mishnah Keritot 1:1

Thirty-six transgressions are punished with excommunication from
the community...compounding the incense used in the Temple for
one's personal use, anointing oneself with the oil of installation used
to consecrate priests, and transgressing the positive commandments of
Pesach and circumcision.

Bavli Megillah 29a

Rav Sheshet (who was blind) was once sitting in the synagogue which
"moved and settled" in Nehardea, when the *Shekhinah* (God's presence)
approached. He did not go out of the synagogue as did the other sages.

The ministering angels came and tried to scare him away.

Rav Sheshet said to God: "Master of the Universe, if one is afflicted and
one is not afflicted, who gives way to whom?"

God then said to the angels: "Let him stay."

Discussion Questions

1. This is the end of the book of Exodus. We've gone from slavery to covenant to sin to wandering. And God has been with us every step of the way. Are there times when you feel God's presence in your life in a constant way? Are there times you feel God is not with you? How do you reconnect?

2. One of the most potent ways of connecting with God was through the incense offered inside the Temple. In addition, people had incense altars in their homes. This is why we have the blessing over spices at Havdalah, the ceremony that ends Shabbat. After Shabbat was over and people could use fire again, they first lit their lamps (hence the blessing over the candle) and then lit their incense. The rising smoke and pleasant scent constituted a sort of direct line to God. How would you use incense to connect to God? Would we benefit by trying to recreate some more of these methods of relating to God that were used in the Temple? Are there some ways of connecting that are truly lost to us? Are there any ways of connecting to God that our ancestors in the desert lacked?

3. Rav Sheshet was in a synagogue in Babylonia built from stones that had been part of the First Temple and had been hauled there after it was destroyed. This was why it was known as the synagogue that had moved (from Israel) and settled (in Babylonia). It was said that God's presence resided in this synagogue as strongly as it had in the Temple. How did Rav Sheshet's apparent disability enable him to encounter God more closely? How can you understand the story metaphorically? Have you ever had the experience of meeting God most potently when you were most vulnerable? What happened?

Chazak, chazak, v'nitchazek
Be strong, strong, and be strengthened!
Hadaran alach! Hadaran alach!
We shall return to you, Mishnah! We shall return to you, Gemara!

When we finish reading a book of the Torah, we affirm how much strength it gives us by reciting the first sentence, above. When we complete a book of Mishnah or Gemara, we vow in Aramaic to return to that book. (We don't have to promise to return to a book of the Torah because we know we will read it again next year.)

Vayikra

SIN

Leviticus 4:1-2

(Moses is instructed regarding the sacrifices.)

And God spoke to Moses saying: Speak to the Israelites saying: A soul which sins by mistake and transgresses any negative commandment and does one of these things which ought not be done....

Mishnah Yoma 8:9

If one says: "I will sin and then repent, I will sin and then repent," an opportunity is not given to him to repent.

If one says: "I will sin and the Day of Atonement will atone for my sin," the Day of Atonement does not bring atonement.

Tosefta Kippurim 4:6-8

One who violates a positive commandment and repents, is forgiven before he moves from his place.... One who violates a negative commandment and repents, repentance suspends the punishment, and the Day of Atonement effects atonement... One who violates a commandment for which the punishment is excommunication from the community or execution, and repents, repentance and the Day of Atonement suspend the punishment, and suffering effects atonement.... But one through whom the Name of Heaven is profaned and who repented, repentance does not have the power to suspend the punishment, nor the Day of Atonement to atone for it, but repentance and the Day of Atonement atone for a third, suffering on the rest of the days of the year atones for a third, and death wipes away the sin.

Discussion Questions

1. The text says, "a soul" which sins, not "a person." What is the difference, if any, between the sin of a soul and the sin of a person? Does it matter if the sin is unintentional?

2. The Mishnah seems to demand honesty. If we know something is a sin, and we do it anyway, we cannot atone. Is this true? Are there ways of atoning even if you know at the start that what you are doing is wrong? How do you stop yourself from sinning?

3. Can suffering have meaning? Can it help you atone for sin? Can it lead you to empathy? How do you understand atonement? Does death wipe away sin? What kind of sins profane the name of heaven?

Tsav

ATONEMENT

Leviticus 8:15

(Moses performs sacrifices as part of the ordination of the Priests.)
And Moses slaughtered the bull that was a sin offering and Moses took
the blood and put it on the horns of the altar, all around with his finger.
This was the sin offering for the altar and Moses soaked the foundation
(*yesod*) of the altar with blood and made it holy, so atonement could be
made by it.

Mishnah Yoma 7:5

The High Priest served in eight articles of clothing and jewelry, while the
regular priest served in four.

Bavli Rosh Hashanah 16b

Three things call a person's sins to be presented before God for
immediate judgment (instead of waiting until Yom Kippur): walking
next to a shaky wall (believing that he has enough merit to keep the wall
from falling on him); being pompous in prayer (believing that he is so
righteous that God will automatically answer his prayers); and calling
down God's judgment upon someone else (which causes God to review
the accuser's record first).

Discussion Questions

1. It has been suggested that in looking at various parts of the Torah (stories, books, law codes), the most important passages can be found in the center. Looking at the five books of the Torah as a whole, one may find in this chapter the mid-point verses, Leviticus 8:8-9; the middle word, *yesod*, "foundation," in our verse; and the middle letter, the aleph in the word *hu* in Leviticus 8:28. What would mean to say that this chapter, in which Aaron is consecrated by Moses as the High Priest, is the center of the Torah?

2. According to *Midrash Rabba* on Leviticus (Tsav 10:6), each of the High Priest's garments atoned for a specific thing. The breastplate, for example, atones for those who pervert justice. Can the grandeur of the synagogue during the High Holidays (e.g., white Torah covers) inspire us to atone for our misdeeds? What do you think motivates people who only attend services on the High Holidays to keep coming back each year?

3. This is one of my favorite pieces of Gemara. In essence, it says, "Don't bring God's scrutiny upon yourself by judging others so harshly, or yourself so leniently." Only a person who is completely righteous could safely walk next to a shaky wall, trusting that his virtue was sufficient to keep the wall from falling on him. What actions might you add to the mishnah's list? Have you ever taken risks because you trusted your own righteousness?

Shemini

INCENSE

Leviticus 10:1-2

(Aaron has offered sacrifices for the first time in the new Tabernacle.)
Nadav and Avihu, the sons of Aaron, each took his censer and put fire in it, and put incense on it and offered strange fire before the Lord, which He had not commanded them to offer. And a fire came out from the Lord and devoured them, and they died before the Lord.

Mishnah Keritot 1:1

There are in the Torah thirty-six transgressions punishable by excommunication: ...when one prepares incense like that used in the Temple....

Bavli Keritot 6a

The incense was made of seventy manehs* each of stact, onycha, galbanum, frankincense; sixteen manehs each of myrrh, cassia, spikenard, and saffron; twelve manehs of costus, three manehs of aromatic bark, and nine manehs of cinnamon. As well as carshina lye, nine kavs†; Cyprus wine, three se'ahs and three kavs; and if he has no Cyprus wine, he may bring old white wine; Sodom salt, a quarter kav; and a bit of smoke-raising ingredient. Rabbi Natan the Babylonian says: Also, a bit of Jordan amber. And if he put honey in it, it is invalid. And if he left out one of the spices, he is liable to the death penalty.

---

* *A maneh is a measure of weight, roughly a pound.*
† *A kav is a unit of volume, roughly a quart. Clearly this is an industrial-sized recipe.*

Discussion Questions

1. As we have seen (Pekudei, page 46), incense is an important but potentially dangerous form of communication with God. We could liken it to your fuse box. You must touch the fuses only in the manner laid out for you. When you stick to the rules, you have electricity for your computer, air conditioner, etc. When you don't stick to the rules, you endanger yourself.* What ways of relating to God are potentially dangerous? How could you manage or minimize this danger?

2. What sins do you think are so bad that, they merit excommunication? What kind of effect, if any, does the exclusion of one person have on the rest of the community?

3. The Gemara records the very recipe we are not to reproduce. In fact, in traditional prayer books, it appears in Shabbat morning services after the hymn *Ein K'Eiloheinu,* and some people read it every day. If we could approximate this mixture, would it be worth the risk to try producing it? Is there a valid place for incense in Jewish ritual?

---

* *True story: I was looking at our fuse box with our contractor. There were some cobwebs in the middle of the fuses and I made to brush them away with my house key. The contractor grabbed my hand just before I would have completed the electrical circuit that would have killed me.*

Tazria

ISOLATION

Leviticus 13:46

(The laws of someone who has scale disease)
All the days during which the plague shall be upon him he shall be unclean. He is unclean. He shall dwell alone (*badad yeisheiv*). His habitation shall be outside the camp.

Mishnah Pirkei Avot 2:4

Hillel said: Do not separate yourself from the community. Do not trust yourself until the day of your death. And do not judge your fellow until you have reached his place. Do not say a thing that cannot be understood at once, trusting that in the end it will be understood. Do not say, "When I have free time I shall study," for perhaps you will not have free time.

Bavli Berachot 63b // Bavli Taanit 7a // Bavli Makkot 10a

The knowledge of Torah is acquired only in group study, as Rabbi Yose said in the name of Rabbi Hanina: What is the meaning of what is written, "A sword is upon the idle talkers (*baddim*) and they shall become fools" (Jeremiah 50:36)? A sword is upon those who hate the students of the sages, that is, those who sit alone (*bad bebad*) and study the Torah. Not only that, they become ignorant through studying alone, i.e., such study does not avail them.

Discussion Questions

1. Does illness isolate us socially? How? Do you find that you are treated as "outsider," or as separate in some way when you are sick?

Are there ways that we can bridge the gap between healthy people and those afflicted with disease?

2. Hillel's teachings balance a sense of immediacy and a sense of deferred gratification. In what ways do we need both? How can you create a healthy balance between these two poles? How does Hillel's teaching here about community connect to his other teachings in this mishnah?

3. The Gemara passage states unequivocally that one must study in community. How do you experience the difference between private study and shared learning? What religious experiences do you prefer to perform with your community? Which privately?

What would be lost and gained if you made your private religious experiences into public ones, and your public experiences into private ones?

Metzora

SCALE DISEASE

Leviticus 14:1-2

(After a lengthy discussion of the disease, we come to instructions for purification.)
The Lord spoke to Moses, saying: This shall be the ritual for a scale-diseased person at the time of his purification, when he shall be brought before the priest.

Mishnah Negaim 2:4

In what posture are people checked for signs of scale disease?

A man is inspected as if hoeing or harvesting olives.

A woman is inspected as if working with dough, or nursing her child, or as if weaving standing, if her right armpit must be inspected. Rabbi Yehudah says, even as if spinning flax, for her left armpit.

Bavli Arakhin 15b-16a

Because of seven things the plague of scale disease is incurred: slander, the shedding of blood, a vain oath, incest, arrogance, robbery, and envy.

Discussion Questions

1. The symptoms of "*Tzara'at*", the skin affliction translated here as "scale disease," do not correspond to any known condition, despite the common translation as "leprosy." The ritual that is described in the Torah text that follows takes place *after* the scale disease is cured. What is the text intimating about God's ability to heal? What does it seem to say about the priest's abilities?

2. The inspection for scale disease must examine some parts of the body that are usually concealed -- but not all of them. The mishnah, then, is giving typical postures, which, because they involve stretching, reveal parts of the body usually concealed. What is fascinating about this mishnah is how it reveals what it considers typical labor for each gender. Do you find that the various roles in your life affect your health in different ways? Do these diverse roles affect how you experience and categorize illness? Do responsibilities make you more or less prone to illness?

3. The sages believed that gossip could lead to disease. *Can* gossip lead to mental, emotional, or physical illness? Are there other immoral actions that you believe could lead to illness? Why or why not? How?

Acharei Mot

FORBIDDEN ACTS

Leviticus 18:5-6

(God instructs the Israelites that they may not follow the ways of the place they have left, Egypt, nor may they follow the ways of the place they are going, Canaan.)
You shall keep my rules and my judgments. If you do so you will live. I am the Lord your God. No one should have intimate relations with any of his close family. I am the Lord.

Mishnah Hagigah 2:1

Three people together should not carefully study the laws of prohibited relationships (Leviticus 18:6-30) . Nor may two people together study the Work of Creation. One person alone may not study the Work of the Chariot, unless he is a sage and understands from his own knowledge.

Bavli Pesachim 25a-b

All forbidden acts may be used to save ourselves except for idolatry, incest and murder.

Discussion Questions

1. These two verses are followed by a long list of sexual taboos. What is the Torah trying to teach us by making this list so explicit and detailed?

2. Are there some subjects that simply shouldn't be mentioned? What if one person very much wants to speak and the other does not want to hear? Is it necessary for both parties to be willing participants in order to discuss something?

Does silence ever serve a constructive purpose? Can it be destructive?

3. Is there something worse than death? Is there something you feel is worth dying for? Is there any part of Judaism which you'd rather die than transgress?

Kedoshim

HOLINESS

Leviticus 19:1-2

The Lord spoke to Moses, saying: Speak to the whole Israelite community and say to them: You shall be holy, for I, the Lord your God, am holy.

Mishnah Kiddushin 1:1

A woman is acquired in three ways... She is acquired with money, with a document (i.e. a marriage contract), and through sexual intercourse.

Bavli Hagigah 16a

Six things are said of human beings: They are like the ministering angels in three ways, and like animals in three ways.

In three ways they are like the ministering angels: They have understanding like the ministering angels, they walk upright like the ministering angels, and they can talk in the holy tongue (Hebrew) like the ministering angels.

In three ways they are like animals: They eat and drink like animals, they have sexual intercourse like animals, and they eliminate waste like animals.

Discussion Questions

1. God tells the Israelites to be holy. What does this command mean to you? What are the ways in which you bring holiness into your life? What does it mean that God is holy?

2. *Kiddushin* (wedding), comes from the same root as *kadosh*, holiness. What does holiness have to do with acquisition? What does holiness have to do with your money? Your word? Your sexuality? What does it have to do with marriage?

3. How are you like an angel? How are you unlike one? Have you ever sensed an angel, a messenger from God, in your life? Have you ever sensed that *you* were filling that role for someone else?

Emor

HARVEST CELEBRATION

Leviticus 23:40

And on the first day of Sukkot you shall take the fruit of goodly trees, branches of palm-trees, and boughs of thick trees, and willows of the brook and you shall rejoice before the Lord your God seven days.

Mishnah Sukkah 5:3

From the worn out undergarments of the priests they made wicks and with them set alight four huge lamps in the Temple forecourt. And there was no courtyard in Jerusalem that was not lit up with the light at the Water-Well Libation ceremony held in the Temple on Sukkot.

Midrash Leviticus Rabbah 30:10

Another exposition of the text, "the fruit of the goodly (*hadar*) tree." *Hadar* symbolizes Abraham, whom the Holy One, blessed be He, honored (*hiddero*) with good old age; as it says, "And Abraham was old, well stricken in age" (Genesis 24:1), and it is written, "And honor (*vehadarta*) the face of the old man" (Leviticus 19:32). "Branches (*kappot*) of palm-trees," symbolizes Isaac who had been tied (*kafut*), and bound upon the altar. "And boughs of thick trees," symbolizes Jacob. Just as the myrtle is crowded with leaves, so was Jacob crowded with children. "And willows of the brook," symbolizes Joseph. Just as the willow wilts before the other three species, so Joseph died before his brothers.

Another explanation of the text, "the fruit of the *hadar* tree." *Hadar* symbolizes Sarah, whom the Holy One, blessed be He, honored (*hidderah*) with a good old age; as it says, "Now Abraham and Sarah were old" (Genesis 18:11). "Branches of palm-trees," symbolizes Rebeccah. Just as the palm-tree contains edible fruit as well as prickles, so Rebeccah brought forth a righteous man (Isaac) and a wicked one (Esau). "And boughs of thick trees," symbolizes Leah. Just as the myrtle is crowded with leaves so was Leah crowded with children. "And willows of the brook," symbolizes Rachel. Just as the willow wilts before the other three species, so Rachel died before her sister.

Discussion Questions

1. How could shaking the *lulav* (the palm frond with willow and myrtle branches) and *etrog* (citron fruit) be a cause to rejoice? How could it be an expression of joy?

2. When the Temple stood in Jerusalem, the highlight of the Sukkot celebration was the joyous Water-Well Libation ceremony. This Mishnah recalls some of the details of the celebration. The innermost garments of the most hidden individuals (i.e., priests), in the most limited-access building (i.e., the Temple), are taken out and burned where everyone can see them! Anthropologists might call this a "ritual of rebellion," wherein a highly role-bound society has one day on which all the roles are reversed. Such rituals serve to defuse communal tension. Do we have any rituals of rebellion today? With the relaxation of role definitions have we lost the need for such rituals?

3. Which one of the four species of the *lulav* do you think symbolizes you? Do you identify with any of the characters from the Torah who correspond to the four species?

If you could pick up four things to present to God to remind Him of your merit, what would you choose?

Behar

SINAI'S VOICE

Leviticus 25:1-2

God spoke to Moses at Mount Sinai, saying: Speak to the Israelites and say to them: When you come to the land which I give to you, let the land rest, a Sabbath for God.

Mishnah Pirkei Avot 6:2

Rabbi Joshua ben Levi said: Every day a heavenly voice goes out from Mount Horev (i.e., Mount Sinai) announcing: Woe to humanity for humiliating Torah. For everyone who does not get busy studying Torah is said to be rebuked.... For there is no freedom except through being busy with studying Torah and anyone who busies himself with Torah study will be praised.

Yerushalmi Shabbat 1:2, 3a

Every Friday afternoon, Rabbi Joshua ben Levi regularly listened to his grandson's reading of the Bible lesson studied during the week....

He who listens to his grandson's reading of Bible is as though he were hearing it at Mount Sinai. For it is said, "Make them known unto your children and your children's children, as if it were the day that you stood before the Lord Your God in Horev." (Deuteronomy 4:9-10)

Discussion Questions

1. Imagine Mount Sinai in all its grandeur and fearsomeness. Now imagine a command issuing forth from that vision saying that you should rest, your animals should rest, and your land should rest. Who, in your life, wields the authority to tell you to ease off, to let go for a while? Do you listen? What is the value of rest?

2. How may Shabbat bring freedom although its practices may seem restrictive? How might Torah study be understood as bringing freedom?

Mount Horev/Sinai is mentioned only four times in the entire Mishnah! What do you make of this paucity of mention?

3. This passage from Gemara teaches that grandparents and grandchildren have the ability to recreate Mount Sinai. That's a lot of power! Did you ever experience this with a grandparent? How have your grandparents or grandchildren helped you to connect to God or to Judaism?

Bechukotai

HUMAN VALUE

Leviticus 27:1-7

And God spoke to Moses saying: Speak to the Israelites and say to them: Whenever a man shall vow the worth of a person to God, then the worth of the male aged 20 to 60 years is 50 silver shekels, and a female of 20 to 60 years old is 30 shekels. And if the person is 5 to 20 years old, a male's value is 20 shekels and a female's is 10. And if the person is between one month and 5 years old, the male is worth 5 shekels, and a female is worth 3 shekels. And if the person is older than 60, a male is worth 15 shekels and a female is worth 10 shekels.

Mishnah Arakhin 1:1 // Sifra Behukotai 8: Parshata 3

All persons are fit to pledge the value of a person or to have their value pledged: priests, Levites, lay Israelites, women, and slaves.

A hermaphrodite (who has indications of both genders) or an androgen (who has indications of neither) are fit to vow another's worth, or to have their worth vowed, and are fit to evaluate, but they are not to be made the subjects of valuation, for the subject of valuation may only be a person definitely male or definitely female.

A deaf-mute person, mentally ill person, or minor are fit to have their worth vowed or be made the subject of valuation, but they are not fit to pledge another's worth or to evaluate, because they have no cognition.

Bavli Sanhedrin 39b

When the Egyptians were killed in the Red Sea, the ministering angels wished to utter the song of praise before the Holy One, blessed be He. But He rebuked them, saying: My handiwork (i.e., the Egyptians) is drowning in the sea. Would you utter a song before me?

Discussion Questions

1. As a symbol of devotion, an Israelite might pledge himself, or a loved one, to God. Such pledges were redeemable through monetary donations to the Temple. The Torah text reflects the relative monetary value of people in that era. Who was worth most? Who was worth least? Do these valuations retain any social or financial meaning for us today? Can we say that some members of our society are worth more than others? How closely do we follow the Torah's valuation system? What do you think would prompt someone to make such a pledge?

2. Since the matter of vowing a person's worth is clearly based on gender in the Torah, those with unclear gender identity could vow someone else's worth, but not be vowed for themselves. The deaf-mute person, mentally ill person, or minor could not make the vow because they were not considered to have cognition. Do we deal any differently today with people who don't fit neatly into categories?

3. The Talmud here teaches that God does not rejoice in the death of even the wickedest of men. From God's perspective, everyone is precious, everyone has worth. Can the ideas of this piece of Gemara be reconciled with those of the Torah and Mishnah ?

Chazak, chazak, v'nitchazek

Be strong, strong, and be strengthened!

Hadaran alach! Hadaran alach!

We shall return to you, Mishnah! We shall return to you, Gemara!

When we finish reading a book of the Torah, we affirm how much strength it gives us by reciting the first sentence, above.

When we complete a book of Mishnah or Gemara, we vow in Aramaic to return to that book. (We don't have to promise to return to a book of the Torah because we know we will read it again next year.)

Bemidbar

COMING OF AGE

Numbers 1:2-3

(God asks Moses to conduct a census)
Take the count of the entire congregation of the Israelites, all the males who go out and make war, who are 20 years old and up, according to their families, and their fathers' houses, by the number of names, head by head.

Mishnah Arachin 2:6

No children could enter the Temple Court to take part in the Service except when the Levites would stand to sing. They did not join in the singing with harp and lyre, but with their voices alone, to add flavor to the music. These minors did not count toward making up the required number of twelve Levites (the minimum needed to sing), nor did they stand on the priestly platform. But they stood on the ground so that their heads could be seen between the legs of the Levites, and they were called "the tormentors of the Levites."

Tosefta Hagigah 1:2

If a minor knows how to wave the *lulav* he is obligated to wave it.

If he knows how to wrap himself in a *tallit* he is obligated to wear *tzitzit* (fringes).

If he knows how to speak, his father teaches him the *Shema* and Torah and the holy language (i.e., Hebrew)....

If he knows how to guard his *tefillin*, his father procures *tefillin* for him.

Discussion Questions

1. According to the Torah text, only those who could fight were counted in this census. Today, what is the standard by which one may "count" as part of the Jewish community? Has our definition broadened?

2. The Levites occupied that twilight space between the mundane world, where all the Israelites lived, and the sacred world of the Temple precincts, where the priests officiated. In anthropology, such a position is called "liminal," i.e., betwixt and between. Who would be considered liminal in the Jewish community today?

3. According to this passage from the Tosefta, one need not be 20, nor even 12 or 13 to begin observing the mitzvot. As soon as one is able to do so, one begins to practice them, bit by bit, until one has gradually reached maturity by the age of puberty. Contrast the priestly need for visible signs of maturity (e.g., full-grown beard) in order to participate in a ritual, with the sages' more flexible view (the ability to perform the tasks). How are each valid today?

Naso

BLESSING

Numbers 6:24-26

(The following are the words with which Aaron and the priests are commanded to bless the people. The notation here reflects the actual composition of the Hebrew phraseology)

God bless-you and-keep-you.

God will-shine His-countenance upon-you and-grace-you.

God will-raise His-countenance upon-you and-give to-you peace.

Mishnah Peah 1:1

These are the things that have no limit: leaving the corners of one's field unharvested; the first fruits offering; appearing in Jerusalem on Sukkot, Pesach and Shavuot; deeds of lovingkindness; and studying Torah.

Bavli Shabbat 127a

These are the things that a person can benefit from in this world and their merit is stored up to their credit in the world to come, namely: honoring parents, deeds of lovingkindness, regularly attending the study house in the morning and the evening, welcoming guests, visiting the sick, preparing the bride for her wedding, burying the dead, sincerely praying and bringing peace between two people.

And the study of Torah is equal to them all.

Discussion Questions

1. The benediction, as written here, is composed of 3, 5 and 7 word lines. Arranged in a pyramid, the middle word of each line would be read, "*Adonai panav elecha*," "God's face is directed toward you." How can God's face be turned toward you? What is God's "face?" How can God's attention be a blessing to you? When might it not be a blessing?

Count how many letters are in each line of the priestly benediction. Then total them all up*. How does this represent that the priestly blessing is pure perfection...the ultimately whole prayer?

2. The traditional prayer book includes this mishnah, as well as the priestly benediction, to be recited as part of daily Torah study. Why do you think they picked this particular mishnah? Does it relate to the priestly benediction? If so, how so?

3. This is the Gemara passage presented for daily study in the prayer book. How is it similar to Mishnah Peah 1:1? How is it different? Are there any deeds whose absence from this list surprises you? Why do you think they might have been excluded?

---

* *Refer back to page viii for a discussion of the significance of the number 60 in the ancient world.*

Behaalotcha

WHEN THE ARK TRAVELED

Numbers 10:35-36

And it came to pass, when the ark traveled, that Moses said: "Rise, God, and let your enemies scatter and let those who hate you flee from before you."

And when the ark would come to rest, Moses would say: "Return, God, to the myriad thousands of Israel."

Mishnah Yadayim 3:5

What is the least amount of writing from a Torah that is still considered a valid piece of Torah? A scroll of the Torah on which the writing has become erased and only 85 letters remain in it (i.e., as many as are in the section which begins, "And it came to pass, when the ark traveled") is a valid Torah text.

Bavli Avodah Zarah 24b

"And it came to pass, when the ark traveled, that Moses said: 'Rise, God...'" What then did the Israelites say? Said Rav Isaac: "Sing, sing ark of acacia wood. Ascend in all your gracefulness, covered with gold. The inner hall of the Temple hears your praise. You are covered with many jewels."

Discussion Questions

1. This passage is bracketed in the Torah with a pair of inverted Hebrew letter *nun*s and is thus considered by the sages to be a whole separate "book."

The image of God hovering over the ark is one of great power: striking fear into those who hate God, and power and pride into those who love God. How does the actual Torah scroll function in this way today?

When you have had occasion to stand before an open Torah, how did you feel? Have you ever experienced a feeling of connection with the generations of people who have read from the scroll before you?

2. The two verses we are studying are the minimum standard for the length of any holy book. If a scroll contains 85 consecutive letters from the Bible, then it is a sacred text. If you took an inventory of your space (home, office, etc.) how many pieces of Torah/Judaica would you find that fit this criteria? Does it change your relationship to these items to think of them as holy texts?

3. According to the Gemara, the Israelites had a responding song they sang when the ark was brought forward and, by extension, when the Torah was taken from the ark. The ark was made from acacia wood and so this song was a hymn describing the glory of the ark. If you were to write a poem or love-song to God, what images might you use?

Shlach L'cha

ON THE FRINGE

Numbers 15:37-41

The Lord said to Moses: Speak to the Israelites and instruct them to make for themselves fringes (*tzitzit*) on the corners of their garments throughout the ages. Let them attach a cord of blue to the fringe at each corner. That shall be your fringe. Look at it and recall all the commandments of the Lord and observe them, so that you do not follow your heart and eyes that could lead you to sin. So shall you be reminded to observe all My commandments and to be holy to your God. I the Lord am your God, who brought you out of the land of Egypt to be your God. I, the Lord, am your God.

Mishnah Menachot 4:1

The absence of the blue in the fringe does not invalidate the white thread nor does the absence of the white thread invalidate the blue thread. The absence of the hand *tefillin* does not invalidate the head *tefillin* nor does the absence of the head *tefillin* invalidate the hand *tefillin**.

Bavli Menachot 43a

Everyone is obligated to wear *tzitzit* (fringes): priests, Levites and Israelites, converts, women and slaves.

---

* More on *tefillin* can be found on page 40.

Discussion Questions

1. Sometimes we need physical tokens to help remind us of who we are and what we should do. This is basically the function of *tzitzit*. Is there any material object you employ to physically remind yourself that you are Jewish? Do you use things such as key chains, Jewish art or necklaces to remind you of your Judaism? Which is the most effective reminder for you? Which best informs others of your Jewish identity?

2. The thread of blue used to be a part of the *mitzvah* of *tzitzit*. Over time, the recipe for the dye was lost and only white threads were used. Recently, the ancient recipe for making this dye has been rediscovered and is currently available. What would the blue and white symbolize for you that the white alone does not?

3. This passage clearly states that women are obligated to wear *tzitzit*. Do you think women should be obligated to wear *tzitizit*? What place does the concept of obligation have in your thinking about Jewish ritual?

Korach
STAFF DEVELOPMENT

Numbers 17:21-23

(After Korach questions Aaron's right to the priesthood, God tells Moses what to do.)
And Moses spoke to the Israelites, and asked that each chief of an ancestral house give him his staff, including Aaron's staff, which was among them. There were 12 staffs in all. Moses placed the staffs before the Lord, in the tent of true witnessing. The next day Moses entered the tent of true witnessing, and Aaron's staff, the staff of the Levites, had sprouted. It had brought forth sprouts, produced blossoms, and even almonds.

Mishnah Pirkei Avot 5:6

Ten things were created on the eve of the Sabbath at twilight, and these are they: the mouth of the earth that swallowed Korach, the mouth of the well of Miriam, the mouth of the talking ass in the story of Bilam and Balak, the rainbow in Noah's story, the manna, the rod of Moses, the *shamir* worm which breaks rocks, the letters, the writing, and the tablets.

Tosefta Yoma 2:15//Bavli Horayot 12a

At the time when the Holy Ark was hidden away prior to Jerusalem's destruction...so was Aaron's rod with its almonds and blossoms.

Discussion Questions

1. In the aftermath of Korach's rebellion, God demonstrates His choice of the house of Aaron by making Aaron's rod bloom and produce almonds. The rods belonging to the other priestly families remained unchanged. Almond, in Hebrew, is *shakeid*, which relates to the idea of wakefulness. (In Israel, the almond tree is the first to flower in the Spring.) How can we be more awake and attentive to God's will in our own lives?

2. Miraculous things, things that are betwixt and between our reality and God's reality, were created in the moment just before the very first Shabbat began. Are there any other things that you might think of that could have been created in this moment? Can borderline times (e.g., nodding off, waking up, coming into and going out of Shabbat) perhaps be some of our most important moments?

3. This is part of a synagogue mosaic floor you can see in Kibbutz Beit Alpha in the Galilee. It is about 1500 years old. You can see a menorah on each side of the ark as well as the lions of Judea and Israel. Right above the lion on the left you can see a somewhat scraggly plant. On the right, in the same position, that plant has fruit and a little bird on top of it. These two plants represent Aaron's rod before and after it flowered. The flowering rod will be taken out of hiding, it is said, when the Temple is rebuilt. What does this symbol mean to you? What do you think it meant to the artisans and worshipers who made this floor?

Hukkat

RED HEIFER

Numbers 19:1-9

God spoke to Moses and to Aaron saying: This is the law of the Torah which God commanded.... Take for yourself a perfect red heifer which has never been made to work with a yoke on its neck.... Take it outside the camp and slaughter it.... Burn the heifer... gather the ashes... for the water of sprinkling, a purification ceremony.

Mishnah Parah 3:1

Seven days before the burning of the red heifer, the priest who was to burn the cow was removed from his house to a chamber facing the northeastern corner of the Temple, called the stone chamber.

Bavli Yoma 2a

The Mishnah teaches that seven days before the Day of Atonement, the high priest was removed from his house.... We learned elsewhere: Seven days before the burning of the red heifer, the priest who was to burn the heifer was removed from his house.

Discussion Questions

1. This cow is not only without blemish, it is free, never having felt a yoke. We take the yoke of heaven on ourselves each day when we say the *Shema*. Why must the cow be free, but we humans must be yoked? What are the roles of freedom and responsibility in our experience of Judaism?

2. What do you think it would be like to experience the purification ritual of being sprinkled with a liquid that includes the red heifer's ashes? What sorts of purification rituals do you practice today (e.g., changing one's clothes, bathing, washing one's hands)? How do such rituals make you feel?

3. This small piece of Gemara is only one part of a long comparison of the rites of the red heifer and the rites of Yom Kippur. Both involve separation, ritual preparation, and perfect specimens (the heifer and the priest must be absolutely blemish-free), and both play enormous roles in repairing possible obstacles between the Jewish people and God. Yom Kippur can also be compared to a more familiar Jewish ritual, namely, a wedding. Torah scrolls are dressed in white on Yom Kippur to symbolize purity. The bride and groom traditionally fast on the day of their wedding. At a wedding, the dress must be perfect (God forbid it gets a stain!), as must be the bride's hair, the food at the reception, etc. How is Yom Kippur, and by extension, the ritual of the red heifer, like a wedding? Is there a way for the Jewish people to "wed" God?

Balak

Numbers 24:5-6

(Bilam has been hired to curse Israel. Instead, he offers this blessing.)
How good are your tents, Jacob, the places where you live, Israel!

Like winding brooks, like gardens on a river's edge,

Like aloes which the Lord planted and cedar trees beside water bodies.

Mishnah Oholot 6:1

A person and utensils can constitute tents which transmit ritual impurity but not tents which can shield from impurity and safeguard ritual purity. How? For example, if four people carry a block of stone and something impure is under it, the items that are on top of the stone become ritually impure.

Bavli Berachot 15b-16a

Why are tents mentioned right alongside streams in this passage of Torah...? To tell you that just as streams raise a person up from a state of impurity to purity, so do tents (i.e., houses of study) raise a person up from the scale of guilt to the scale of merit.

Discussion Questions

1. The prophet Bilam was supposed to curse the Israelites, and instead ended up blessing them. Why do you think these words have become the first phrases we recite upon entering a synagogue? Is there something to be learned from its original context here in the Torah?

Notice how the first part of a verse is echoed or amplified in the second part of a verse of poetry. One of the biggest stumbling blocks to appreciating biblical poetry is understanding the use of parallelism. In most biblical poetry, the first part of the verse is echoed in some way in the second part of the verse. Does this insight help you to better understand Psalms and other Hebrew poetry?

2. In the Mishnah, "tent" can denote any enclosed, covered space (even a temporary one, as in this mishnah), that can cast a shadow over a corpse. It is within this space that impurity may be transmitted. This long tractate of the Mishnah conveys the idea that a soul, when liberated from the body, creates an impurity (*tumah*). The rabbis thought this *tumah* could enter anything that interfered with its path which went straight up to the sky and straight down...somewhat like a laser beam. What might this image have meant to the sages? Have you ever sensed this impurity related to death?

What do *you* think happens to your soul after you die?

3. The Gemara sees tents as study houses. The conceptual focus is thereby diverted from ritual purity to moral uprightness. What are the tents that bless the Jewish community today? Synagogues? JCCs? Federations? Day schools? Books? Web pages? Or is it wherever Torah or charity reside?

Pinchas

IDOLATRY

Numbers 25:17-18

(God speaks to Moses after punishing the idolatrous Israelites.)
Give the Midianites trouble and attack them. For they gave you trouble with their nonsense, with which they beguiled you in the matter of Peor and in the affair of Kozbi, the daughter of a prince of Midian, their sister.

Mishnah Avodah Zarah 4:7

The Elders (Rabban Gamliel, Rabbi Elazar ben Azariah, Rabbi Yehoshua ben Hananiah and Rabbi Akiba, who went to Rome in 95 C.E.) were asked: "If Your God does not want idolatry, why does He not abolish it?"

The Elders said to the Romans: "If it was something unnecessary to the world that was worshiped, He would abolish it. But people worship the sun, moon, stars and planets. Should He destroy His universe on account of fools?"

The Romans said to the Elders: "If so, He should destroy what is unnecessary for the world and leave what is necessary for the world!"

The Elders said to the Romans: "If He did that, we should merely be strengthening the hands of idol worshipers. They would say: 'Know that these things (e.g., the sun or stars) are surely gods, for behold they have not been destroyed!'"

Bavli Avodah Zarah 35b

One time Rabbi Yehudah the Prince went out into a field, and an idolater brought before him a loaf baked in a large oven from about two gallons of flour.

Rabbi Yehudah the Prince said: "How beautiful is this bread! Why did the sages prohibit us from eating it?"

Why should the sages have thought fit to prohibit eating it?! Because of intermarriages!

Discussion Questions

1. The Midianite women seduced the Israelites and caused them to worship the Midianite gods. Have you ever been in a relationship that caused you to be untrue to your best self? How can you extricate yourself from such a relationship?

2. This mishnah asks, "Why doesn't God eliminate idolatry?" Destroying the world as a punishment for idolatry is not a possibility since God promised Noah after the flood that He would not destroy the world again. Has idolatry, as it was practiced in the time of the Mishnah, been destroyed? If so, what has taken its place? Have the Elders' prayers been answered? Have the questions of the Romans been answered?

3. The loaf that Rabbi looked at was an enormous ceremonial bread and he was tempted to partake of its beauty and tastiness. How would intermarriages be prevented by avoiding the bread of idol worshipers? How does keeping kosher help maintain one's Jewish identity? Is there any other practice as potent? How does keeping kosher relate to any other personal food issues you may have?

Mattot

POWER

Numbers 30:9

If a man heard his wife make a vow, he can disavow that promise she made on pain of her soul; and it will be null and void and the Lord will forgive her.

Mishnah Ketubot 5:6

If a husband vowed not to have sexual intercourse with his wife, the School of Shammai says he must divorce her within two weeks while the School of Hillel says he must divorce her in one week....

How often are husbands required to offer to have sexual intercourse with their wives? Men who do not do physical labor, every day. Men who do physical labor, twice a week. Mule drivers, once a week. Camel drivers, once a month. Sailors, once every six months.

Bavli Gittin 34a

Giddal bar Re'ilai sent a *get* (a divorce decree) to his wife. The bearer went and found her weaving. He said to her: "Here is your *get*."

She said to him: "Go away now since, as you see, my hands are all tied up in the loom and I cannot receive the document properly. So come again tomorrow."

The messenger returned to Giddal and told him what happened, whereupon he said: "Blessed is He who is good and does good!"

Discussion Questions

1. According to one interpreter of Numbers (anthropologist Mary Douglas), women in the book of Numbers represent Israel and their husbands represent God. In this context, how do you understand the ability of a husband to nullify a wife's vow? Is it an act of power? An act of mercy? Does the ability to take back your words have value for you, personally? Would there be a value in having someone else with the power to take your words back for you (especially in this era of instant reply by email or fax)?

2. In the sages' system, a husband had the duty of offering to have sexual intercourse with his wife. If he broke that contract by vowing not to fulfill this duty, his wife could force him to divorce her and pay her the divorce settlement. In the sages' system the divorce settlement was set up at the time of marriage, when the man wanted the woman the most, not at the time of divorce (as in America) when the husband would want the woman the least. How does the sages' system benefit women and men? How does work effect one's marital life?

3. As we can see from this passage, men also had chances to take back rash words and actions. A divorce does not take effect until the document—the *get* – is received by the wife. This rabbi was known for his fiery temper and one gets the impression that he has tried to divorce his wife in a fit of anger before. Have you ever been able to dismiss another person's anger and rash actions to such good effect? How did you manage to remain unprovoked?

Mas'ei

FORESIGHT

Numbers 35:10-11

Speak to the Israelites and say to them: When you come over the Jordan to the land of Canaan, create for yourselves cities of refuge, so that one who kills another accidentally can flee to one of these cities.

Mishnah Pirkei Avot 3:20

Everything is given on credit and a net is spread over everything that lives so that no one can escape God's system. The store is open and the storekeeper gives credit. The ledger is open and the hand writes. Whoever wishes to borrow can do so but they should know that the collectors come punctually, and extract payment from everyone, whether they want to pay or not.

Bavli Menachot 29b

When Moses went up to receive the Torah from the Holy One, blessed be He, he found Him occupied, putting crowns on the letters.

Said Moses: "Lord of the Universe, why are You doing this tedious work?"

God answered: "A man named Akiba ben Joseph will come who will read great meaning into all these little crowns."

Moses said: "Master of the Universe, may I see him?"

God said: "Turn and look!"

Moses went and sat down in a study session taught by Rabbi Akiba. He sat at the very back of the room and he could not understand anything of what was said. Moses began to feel very low until he heard one of the students ask Rabbi Akiba how he knew something and Rabbi Akiba said: "Because it is a teaching given to Moses on Mount Sinai."

When Moses turned back to the Holy One blessed be He, he asked: "Master of the Universe, why do You give the Torah to me when you could give it to such a greater man?"

God replied: "Shhh. This is My decision."

Discussion Questions

1. This verse from Torah tells us to prepare for things that may never occur. Imagine what it would be like, building a city, hoping it would remain empty. Would it be like all the generations of families who ended their seders with the words, "Next year in Jerusalem!" knowing they would never have the chance to see Jerusalem?

 What does this teach us about having the long view of history: God's perspective, if you will?

2. In today's credit-driven world, this mishnah has greater meaning than ever. How can understanding God and God's creation through this economic metaphor help you see another aspect of creation?

3. Here is another example of God's point of view as opposed to ours. Moses clearly sees Rabbi Akiba as superior to himself (not surprisingly since Moses shows low self-esteem throughout the Torah). Yet God gives Moses, not Rabbi Akiba, the Torah. Why might that be?

What does it say of God's longer view that He places the crowns on the Torah's letters hundreds of years before they will be understood?

Chazak, chazak, v'nitchazek

Be strong, strong, and be strengthened!

Hadaran alach! Hadaran alach!

We shall return to you, Mishnah! We shall return to you, Gemara!

When we finish reading a book of the Torah, we affirm how much strength it gives us by reciting the first sentence, above.

When we complete a book of Mishnah or Gemara, we vow in Aramaic to return to that book. (We don't have to promise to return to a book of the Torah because we know we will read it again next year.)

Dvarim

PROTECTION

Deuteronomy 3:22

(Moses addresses the people as they prepare to enter the Land of Israel.)
You shall not fear the nations that surround you, for the Lord your God is the one who fights for you.

Mishnah Sanhedrin 2:4

The king writes a Torah scroll for himself. When he goes out to war he takes it with him, and when he returns, the scroll returns with him. And when he sits in judgment it is with him, and when he sits down to eat it is before him, as it is said, "And it shall be with him, and he shall read it, all the days of his life" (Deuteronomy 17:19).

Bavli Sanhedrin 97b

The world must contain no fewer than thirty-six righteous people in each generation who have been welcomed into God's most intimate Divine Presence, for it is written, "Blessed are they who wait for Him" (Isaiah 30:18), and the Hebrew word *lo*, meaning "for him," has the numerical value of 36.

Discussion Questions

1. Since God promises military victory to the Israelites, they should not fear. How does our fear lead to our own defeat? Does fear prevent you from doing what you feel destined to do?

2. The king of Israel was to have a Torah scroll with him at all times. Can Torah improve your judgment? Can better judgment make you less fearful? Do you feel that Torah has a protective quality?

3. The sages envision righteous people acting as "living Torah scrolls," protecting communities by their very presence. In what way do you think this may be true?

The largest Jewish court, the Great Sanhedrin, consisted of 71 sages, so 36 would comprise a majority. Can one person tip the balance toward righteousness in a community? Do you know of any such people?

Va'etchanan
SHEMA YISRAEL

Deuteronomy 6:4-5

Hear O Israel, the Lord our God, the Lord is one. You shall love the Lord your God with all your heart and with all your soul and with all your might.

Mishnah Berachot 1:1

From what time may one recite the *Shema* in the evening?

Rabbi Eliezer says: From the time that the priests enter their houses in order to eat their *terumah* offering until the end of the first watch. The sages say: Until the middle of the middle watch. Rabban Gamaliel says: Until the dawn breaks.

Bavli Berachot 61b

When they took Rabbi Akiba out for execution, it was the time of day to recite the *Shema*. While they raked his flesh with iron combs, he recited the first line of the Shema, taking upon himself the yoke of the kingship of heaven.

His students said to him: "Our teacher, you are faithful even to this point of torture?"

Rabbi Akiba said to them: "All my days I have been troubled by this verse, 'You shall love the Lord your God... with all your soul', which I interpret as, 'You should love Him even if He takes your soul.' When shall I have the opportunity of fulfilling this? Now that I have the opportunity shouldn't I fulfill this mitzvah? Rabbi Akiba prolonged the word *echad* (one) until he died while saying it.

A heavenly voice proclaimed: "Happy are you, Akiba, that your soul has departed with the word *echad*!"

The ministering angels said before the Holy One, blessed be He: "Is this Torah, and is this its reward?"

... A heavenly voice went forth and proclaimed: "Happy are you, Rabbi Akiba, that you are destined for the life of the world to come."

Discussion Questions

1. The *Shema* is not just about God being one; it is about each of us being at one with God (i.e. loving God). Is being at one with God possible? Why do you think reciting *Shema* is considered "accepting the yoke of the kingship of Heaven"? What is the connection between the unity of God and the love of God?

2. Jewish days begin at evening. Not until nightfall could priests purify themselves (by immersing in a *mikveh* bath) in order to eat *terumah,* the food donations which were a major source of their sustenance. Why do you think the mishnah connects our recitation of the *Shema* to the priests' purification?

The watches referred to each represent a third of the night, so the sages are debating whether the *Shema* can be recited as soon as the sun sets, half of the night, or up until the break of dawn? Why do you think it makes a difference?

Can our words affect God's actual unity? What do you make of the requirement to unify God twice daily?

3. Rabbi Akiba teaches us how to give meaning to our pain. His experience of pain is alleviated because he finds meaning in it. Is it possible for us to give our pain context and meaning?

Eikev

GRACE

Deuteronomy 8:10

When you have eaten and are satisfied, then you shall bless the Lord your God for the good land that He has given you.

Mishnah Berakhot 7:2

Women, children and slaves may not be counted toward the three people needed to say the invitation for grace after meals.

Bavli Pesachim 119b

The Holy One, blessed be He, will make a great banquet for the righteous when the messianic era begins. After they have eaten and drunk, God will ask Abraham to say the invitation for the grace after meals. But he will refuse, saying: "I am not worthy to say the invitation because I was father to Ishmael."

Then Isaac will be asked, but he will say: "I am not worthy because I was father to Esau."

Then Jacob will be asked, but he will say: "I am not worthy because I married two sisters during both their lifetimes and the Torah was destined to forbid such relationships."

Then Moses will be asked, but he will say: "I am not worthy because I did not merit entrance to the Land of Israel either in death or in life."

Then Joshua will be asked, but he will say: "I am not worthy because I did not have a son."

Finally, David will be asked, and he will say: "I will do the invitation to say grace and it is fitting that I do so!"

Discussion Questions

1. The Torah rarely commands us to say words. Why does the Torah make an exception in requiring a blessing after meals?

2. Before grace is said, three men together (or three women together) can do a "call and response" invitation (*zimmun*) to begin the grace. The Mishnah excludes women, children, and slaves from this practice. These three categories of people are considered liminal in the eyes of the Mishnah; that is, not quite in, but not quite out, of the sages' society. What are the determining factors you employ to decide who belongs in a group?

3. I don't know about you, but my jaw dropped the first time I read this passage. David? David-the-adulterer-who-arranged-to-have-the-husband-killed feels worthy when Abraham and Moses do not? But the Gemara teaches a valuable lesson. The greatest person present is the one that is supposed to say the invitation to grace but low self-esteem stopped these people from doing so. When have you let low self-esteem get in the way of your enjoying life and accepting honors?

What do you imagine various biblical women would say in this situation?

R'eh

IDOLS

Deuteronomy 13:18-19

You will not keep one single thing related to idolatry, so that the Lord may turn from fierce anger and show you mercy and compassion and multiply your numbers just as He swore to your fathers he would do, when you shall listen to the voice of the Lord your God and keep all His commandments which I command you this day, and do that which is right in the eyes of the Lord your God.

Mishnah Avodah Zarah 3:1

All images are prohibited because they are worshiped once a year. These are the words of Rabbi Meir.

But the sages say: An image is not prohibited except one that has a staff or bird or orb in its hand.

Rabban Shimon ben Gamliel says: Any image which has anything in its hand is prohibited.

Bavli Avodah Zarah 41b

If an idol was broken of its own accord, Rabbi Yohanan said that its fragments are prohibited and Rabbi Shimon ben Lakish said that they are permitted.

Rabbi Yohanan said that they are prohibited because the idol has not been annulled.

Rabbi Shimon ben Lakish said that they are permitted because the owner certainly annuls the idol without expressly doing so by saying: It could not save itself, so how can it save me?

Discussion Questions

1. Imagine a world filled with idols, like ancient Greece or Rome. Could one possibly hope to destroy them all? Should one?

2. What do you think is special about images holding a staff, a bird, or an orb?

Look around. Do you have any objects with images, especially images of people with things in their hands (e.g., the Columbia Pictures logo on a DVD or the Statue of Liberty)? How do you relate this mishnah to your own belongings?

3. The Gemara focuses on the relationship between a person and his idol. Idolaters worshiped power. Once the power was demonstrably gone, the object was no longer worthy of worship and was nullified for purposes of idolatry. We nullify our *chametz* (leavened products) at Pesach. Can you imagine applying this power of nullification to other areas of life which you consider negative?

Shoftim

JUSTICE

Deuteronomy 16:20

Justice, only justice, shall you pursue, that you may live and inherit the land which the Lord your God gives you.

Mishnah Sanhedrin 4:5

How did the judges exhort the witnesses in capital cases? They were reminded of the sacredness of each life and of their duty when the judges spoke to them as follows: "...Only one single person was created first, to teach you that anyone who causes a soul to be lost from humanity, the Torah counts it as if he had destroyed the whole world. And anyone who sustains a single soul of humanity, the Torah counts it as if he had sustained the whole world."

Bavli, Avodah Zarah 52a

Whoever appoints an unworthy judge is as though he plants an *asheirah* in Israel, as it is said, "Judges and officers shall you make you in all your gates." (Deuteronomy 16:18), and near it is written, "You shall not plant an *asheirah* of any kind" (Deuteronomy 16:21).

Rav Ashi said: If he appointed such a judge in a place where there are students of the sages, it is as though he had planted an *asheirah* by the side of the altar.

Discussion Questions

1. Why do you think the word "justice" is doubled? Why does justice lead to inheritance of the land?

2. How would the Mishnah's exhortation, delivered to witnesses in a capital case, act as a deterrent to false testimony? Would such a warning work in a court today? In what other contexts could you envision this exhortation being fruitfully used?

3. An *asheirah* is an idolatrous cult item made of wood (possibly a tree). The prohibition against the *asheirah* appears next to the verses in the Torah about setting up a fair justice system. From this juxtaposition, the sages learn that the two things are related. Which *asheirot* (e.g., money, power, status) do you find particularly appealing? How could you cleanse your own altar and place a "true judge/sage" in its place?

Ki Teitzei

REMEMBER

Deuteronomy 25:17-18

(Tradition teaches that Haman was a descendant of Amalek. Accordingly, this piece of Torah is read in the synagogue on the Shabbat before Purim.)

Remember what Amalek did to you when you were coming out of Egypt; how he took you by surprise and struck the stragglers and those who were most feeble, who trailed behind the rest of the group because they were tired and faint. And he did not fear God.

Mishnah Megillah 1:8

The only difference between holy books and *tefillin* and *mezuzahs* is that the holy books may be written in any language, while *tefillin* and *mezuzahs* can only be written in Hebrew.

Rabban Shimon ben Gamliel says: Even holy books can be written in any language, but the sages did not allow holy books to be written in any language aside from Hebrew except Greek.

Bavli Megillah 7b

It is the duty of a man to mellow himself with wine on Purim until he cannot tell the difference between "cursed be Haman," *(arur Haman),* and "blessed be Mordecai," *(baruch Mordecai).*

Discussion Questions

1. Amalek attacked the Israelites in a vicious way as they were leaving Egypt. Why must we remember this? What good does it do to us to remember this? What harm, if any, does it do to remember this?

2. For the Mishnah, "holy books" means the Torah and other Biblical scrolls. (The Mishnah and other early rabbinic texts were transmitted orally, representing the Oral Torah.) How would it change the Torah reading, or the reading of the *Megillah* on Purim, if English scrolls were read in the synagogue? Would it improve the experience? What would be lost by not reading in Hebrew? Which way do you think is better?

3. Time for some *gematria**:
In what way are cursing Mordecai and blessing Haman equivalent?

Arur Haman (ארור המן) =   *Baruch Mordecai* (ברוך מרדכי) =

aleph (א)	= 1 +		bet (ב)	= 2 +
reish (ר)	= 200 +		reish (ר)	= 200 +
vav (ו)	= 6 +		vav (ו)	= 6 +
reish (ר)	= 200 +		caf (ך)	= 20 +
hey (ה)	= 5 +		mem (מ)	= 40 +
mem (מ)	= 40 +		reish (ר)	= 200 +
nun (ן)	= 50 +		dalet (ד)	= 4 +
			caf (כ)	= 20 +
= 502			yud (י)	= 10

= 502

In what way are they different? Why do you think these two phrases are equal in *gematria*? Keeping in mind that alcohol can inhibit one's memory, what do you make of the obligation to become intoxicated on Purim, particularly in light of the Torah's commandment to "remember"?

---

* *See page viii for a brief introduction to this form of numerology.*

Ki Tavo
FIRST FRUITS

Deuteronomy 26:5
(When one came to bring first fruits to the priest, he brought his basket before the priest and said the following words:)
My father was a wandering Aramean, and he went down to Egypt and sojourned there with a few men and became there a great, copious, numerous nation.

Mishnah Bikkurim 3:6-7
While the basket of first fruits was still on his shoulder he would recite from, "I profess this day unto the Lord your God" (Deuteronomy 26:3), until the completion of the passage (Deuteronomy 26:10).

Rabbi Judah said: When he reached the sentence, "My father was a wandering Aramean," he took the basket off his shoulder and held it by its edge and the priest placed his hand beneath it and waved it. The Israelite then recited from, "My father was a wandering Aramean," until he completed the entire passage. He would then deposit the basket by the side of the altar, bow deeply and leave.

Originally, everyone who knew how to recite the whole paragraph (Deuteronomy 26:3-10) would recite it, while those who could not say it from memory repeated it phrase by phrase after the priest. But when people stopped bringing first fruits because they couldn't recite the passage, it was decided that everyone would repeat the declaration phrase by phrase after the priest.

Passover Haggadah
"My father was a wandering Aramean." He was impelled, by force of the Divine word, as it is written, "Know for a certainty that your offspring shall be strangers in a strange land and they shall be enslaved and afflicted for four hundred years" (Genesis 15:13).

Discussion Questions

1. This is the first line of a "capsule history" of the Jewish people. If you were to formulate a continuation of this capsule history until the present, how would you phrase it? Which persons from Jewish history would you include?

2. Why is the gift of the first fruits incomplete without the recitation of Jewish history? What does the story add to the bringing of first fruits?

What do you make of this mishnah's ruling allowing those who could not recite the passage to save face?

3. Going to Egypt can function as a metaphor for going to a place of slavery in one's life. Why would God send the Jewish people, or you yourself, to such a place? What is there to be learned in Egypt?

Nitzavim
CLOSE AND PERSONAL

Deuteronomy 30:11, 14

For that which I command you this day is not hidden from you nor is it far off.... But the word is very near to you, in your mouth and in your heart so that you may do it.

Mishnah Pirkei Avot 1:14

If I am not for myself, who will be? But when I am for myself, what am I? And if not now, when?

Bavli Eruvin 54b

Rabbi Prida had a student whom he taught his lesson 400 times before the latter could master it.

One day, as Rabbi Prida was teaching this student, a person entered and asked Rabbi Prida to help him when he was done teaching. Rabbi Prida agreed and then continued teaching but the student could not master the material.

Rabbi Prida asked: "Why are you having such a hard time today?"

The student said: "Ever since that man came in, I've been sure you'll get up and leave."

Rabbi Prida said: "Come, I will teach it to you again from the beginning."

At that, a voice came out of heaven and said: "Rabbi Prida, which reward would you like...that you live for 400 years or that your whole generation be admitted into the World to Come?"

Rabbi Prida said: "I would like my whole generation to be admitted into the World to Come."

The Holy One, blessed be He, said: "Give him both rewards!"

Discussion Questions

1. When have the commandments felt very far away from you? When have they felt near?

2. This is one of the best known pieces from the Mishnah. It has so many possible meanings. Does it mean that when I am for myself I become nothing? Or when I'm only for myself I become...? And what is it that needs doing now and not later?

3. How accessible were the words of Torah to Rabbi Prida? To his student? What does this story tell us about the sages' attitude toward learning differences?

Should the student get some credit for being willing to sit through a lesson not 400 times, but 800 times?

Vayelech

DEATH

Deuteronomy 31:14

And God said to Moses: The days of your death are approaching.

Mishnah Berachot 2:6

Rabban Gamliel washed on the first night after his wife died. His students said to him: Our teacher, you taught us that a mourner is forbidden to wash. He said to them: I am not like others, for I am fastidious.

Yerushalmi Berachot 2:7

Once some sages were sitting discussing Torah under a certain fig tree. Each day the owner of the fig tree would awaken early and gather the ripe figs. They said: "Perhaps he suspects that we are taking his figs. Let us change our place."

The next day the owner of the fig tree came and said to them: "My masters, you have deprived me of one of the commandments (aiding Torah study) which you used to fulfill under my tree."

The sages said to him: "We feared perhaps you suspected us of taking your figs."

The next morning he thought he would let them see why he picked the figs early. He waited until the sun shone upon them and his figs became worm-eaten.

At that time they said: "The owner of the fig tree knows when it is the right time to pick a fig and he picks it at that time. So, too, God knows when it is the right time to take righteous persons from the world, and at that time He takes them."

Discussion Questions

1. God tells Moses that his life is near its end. How does God tell people that it is time to die? Can you see death as a gift rather than as a punishment; a rest rather than a relegation to the dust?

2. Rabban Gamliel demonstrates here that the rules of mourning may be customized, so to speak, to suit the needs of the mourner. Which rules of mourning would you customize?

3. There is a time to be born and a time to die. Does God's method of gathering souls make sense to you? Does it make more sense after some time has passed after the death of someone dear? Or does it remain an unsolved mystery?

Ha'azinu

LEAVETAKING

Deuteronomy 32:4

(Moses addresses a final, poetic speech to the nation of Israel before his death.)
The Rock! His deeds are perfect; and all His ways are just.
A faithful God without sin; righteous and straightforward is He.

Mishnah Sanhedrin 10:1

All Israel have a portion in the world to come.... And these are they who have no share in the world to come: the one that says that the principle of the resurrection of the dead is not from the Torah, and that the Torah is not from Heaven.

Bavli Avodah Zarah, 17b

The Romans then brought up Rabbi Hanina ben Teradion and they said to him: "Why have you occupied yourself with Torah which the emperor had forbidden under penalty of death?"

The rabbi said to them: "Thus the Lord my God commanded me." At once they sentenced him to be burnt....

As he went out from the tribunal he accepted the righteousness of the Divine righteous judgment. He quoted, "The Rock, His work is perfect; for all his ways are justice" (Deuteronomy 32:4)....

They took hold of him, wrapped him in the Scroll of the Law, placed bundles of branches round him and set them on fire. They then brought tufts of wool, which they had soaked in water, and placed them over his heart, so that he should die slowly.

His daughter said to him: "Father, that I should see you in this state!"

He said to her: "If it were I alone being burnt it would have been a thing hard for me to bear. But now that I am burning together with the Scroll of the Law, He who will have regard for the plight of the Torah will also have regard for my plight."

His students said to him: "Rabbi, what do you see?"

He said to them: "The parchments are being burnt but the letters are flying free...."

The executioner said to him: "Rabbi, if I raise the flame and take away the tufts of wool from over your heart, will you assure me that I will enter into the life to come?"

The rabbi said to him: "Yes."

The executioner said to him: "Then swear unto me."

He swore to him that he would enter the world to come. The executioner immediately raised the flame and removed the tufts of wool from over his heart, and his soul quickly departed. The executioner then jumped and threw himself into the fire. And a heavenly voice went forth saying: "Rabbi Hanina ben Teradion and the executioner are destined for life in the world to come."

When Rabbi heard it he wept and said: "There are those who acquire eternity in one hour, and then there are those who acquire eternity over many years!"

Discussion Questions

1. How is God a rock for you? What other metaphorical images might you use to describe God's presence in your life?

2. According to the Mishnah's criteria, will you merit life in the world to come? What sinners do you think God should exclude from the world to come? Are there any beliefs that you think should exclude people from being called part of "Israel"?

3. Rabbi Hanina ben Teradion accepts his fate serenely. What does that image mean to you? How could you experience "the letters flying free" in your life? Is there a qualitative difference between the eternal life acquired in an hour, or that acquired over the course of a lifetime? Which is easier? Is it fair to be able to employ a "shortcut" in this matter?

V'zot Habrachah

GOD'S KISS

Deuteronomy 34:7

Moses was 120 years old when he died and his vision was not dimmed, nor was his manly vigor abated.

Mishnah Sotah 9:15

Zeal leads to purity, purity leads to selectedness, selectedness leads to holiness, holiness leads to modesty, modestly leads to the fear of sin, the fear of sin leads to righteousness, righteousness leads to the holy spirit, the holy spirit leads to the resurrection of the dead, resurrection of the dead leads to the coming of Elijah, may his memory be for good. Amen.

Deuteronomy Rabbah 11:10

God said: Moses, shut your eyes. And Moses did so. He then said: Put your hands on your chest. And Moses did so. He then said: Put your feet next to each other. And Moses did so.... Then God took Moses' soul with a kiss.

Discussion Questions

1. Moses apparently showed no signs of aging, right up till his death. Why might that be? Why do you think this was such an important point for us to know?

2. This mishnah shows us, step by step, how, by continuing to push ourselves upward in a spiral of holiness, we can each individually help to bring about the messianic era. What do you think about the emphasis on individual accomplishment? Is the principle of "start with yourself" a good one when we seek to improve the world?

3. Even as great a leader Moses must die. Just as God took Miriam's soul with a kiss (Bavli Moed Katan 28a), so God took Moses' soul from his body with a kiss. Have you ever known of a death that was so easy, tender and merciful that you could think of it as if it were a kiss from God? What happened? How would you envision such a death?

Chazak, chazak, v'nitchazek

Be strong, strong, and be strengthened!

Hadaran alach! Hadaran alach!

We shall return to you, Mishnah! We shall return to you, Gemara!

When we finish reading a book of the Torah, we affirm how much strength it gives us by reciting the first sentence, above.

When we complete a book of Mishnah or Gemara, we vow in Aramaic to return to that book. (We don't have to promise to return to a book of the Torah because we know we will read it again next year.)

Rosh Hashanah
SUCKLING CHILDREN

Genesis 21:7-8

And Sarah said: Who would have said to Abraham that Sarah should give children suck? For I have borne him a son in his old age. And the child grew and was weaned. And Abraham made a great feast on the same day that Isaac was weaned.

Mishnah Ketubot 5:5

These are the tasks that a wife performs for her husband: she grinds grain, bakes, launders, cooks, nurses her child, makes his bed, and works with wool. If she brought one maidservant with her into the marriage, she does not grind, bake, nor launder. If she brought two, she does not cook nor nurse her child. If she brought three, she does not make his bed nor work with wool. If she brought four maidservants with her into the marriage, she sits in a chair at her leisure.

Bavli Ketubot 60a

There was a certain divorced woman who came before Shmuel because she did not want to nurse her child anymore.... Shmuel said: "Go and test her."

Shmuel went and placed her in a row of women, and took her son and passed him before them. When the child reached her, he looked up at her face. She hid her eyes from him.

Shmuel said to her: "Raise your eyes, stand up, and take your child."

Discussion Questions

1. This weaning feast of Isaac's is the only weaning celebration recorded in the entire Bible. Do you know of weaning feasts current in Jewish or other cultures that might shed light on this ritual? If you were to create such a celebration today, what would it entail?

What connection does the developmental step of weaning have with spiritual progress as measured on Rosh Hashanah?

2. According to the mishnah, a wife's housework, which includes nursing, has monetary value. How does the Jewish concept of marriage—based on responsibilities agreed to before the contract is entered into—differ from other modern conceptions of marriage? How does this mirror our relationship with God?

3. The divorced woman in the Gemara passage does not want to nurse her child. Since she is no longer married, she does not have to perform this marital obligation. However, the sages (correctly) believed that once a child became used to the experience and taste of his mother's milk, he would not nurse from another woman. So Shmuel devises an experiment to see if the child already recognizes its mother. The child does and so, even though divorced and not obligated by her wedding contract to nurse the child, she must still do so to save the child's life. How is this metaphor of the woman unwilling to nurse her own child related to the ways we take responsibility for things, or not? Does it connect to how we evaluate ourselves at this time of "an accounting of the soul?"

Yom Kippur

LIKE THE ANGELS

Leviticus 16:2

And God said to Moses: Speak to your brother Aaron and tell him that at no time should he enter the holy area behind the curtain before the covering on the ark or he will die because I, God, appear in the smoke above the covering on the ark.

Mishnah 8:1

On the Day of Atonement it is forbidden to eat, drink, wash, anoint, put on sandals and have sexual intercourse.

Rabbi Eliezer said: But a king and a bride may wash their faces and a woman in childbirth may wear sandals.

The sages, however, prohibited such activities on the Day of Atonement.

Bavli Menachot 110a

"This is an ordinance for ever to Israel..." (II Chronicles 2:3). This refers to the altar built in Heaven upon which Michael, the Great Prince of Angels, stands and offers offerings.

Discussion Questions

1. On the Day of Atonement a man with perfect lineage, in perfect clothes, in a state of perfect ritual purity, *still* had to be very careful not to come too close to God's presence. Have you ever come very close to God's presence? Have you ever been in a position where you feared for your life? In your experience—or imagination—are the feelings the same, or different?

2. On Yom Kippur we are to try to be as much like the angels as possible. One way we accomplish this is by becoming more like them physically. As we saw in Kedoshim (page 60), the angels don't eat or drink. How else could you make yourself feel more like an angel on Yom Kippur?

3. The sages believed that everything on earth had a heavenly corollary. So when the priests offered up the sacrifices on earth, Michael offered them on high, as well. In what other ways do Yom Kippur services evoke a heavenly counterpart? Will you behave differently during services knowing that you have a counterpart in heaven?

Sukkot

HOLIDAY OBSERVANCE

(see also Emor, p.62)

Leviticus 23:40

And on the first day of the festival you shall take the fruit of goodly trees, branches of palm trees, boughs of thick trees, and willows of the brook, and you shall rejoice before the Lord your God for seven days.

Mishnah Sukkah 2:3

One who makes his *sukkah* on top of a wagon or on a boat has made an acceptable *sukkah*.... One who makes a *sukkah* on top of a tree or on a camel's back has made an acceptable *sukkah*.

Bavli Sukkah 2b

A *sukkah* which is higher than twenty cubits (more than 30 feet) is not valid, but Rabbi Yehudah declared it valid up to a height of forty or fifty cubits.

Rabbi Yehudah said, "It happened that Queen Helena in Lydda had a *sukkah* that was higher than twenty cubits and the elders nevertheless were going in and out of it and spoke not a word to her in disagreement."

Discussion Questions

1. The four species of the *lulav* (citron, palm, myrtle and willow) all have symbolic significance. If you were to make an "American *lulav*" of plants that represented four important things about you, what plants would you pick? For example, you could include a pine branch (or pine cone) as it is "ever green" to symbolize your hope that your love of Judaism would be evergreen.

2. You could almost make a Dr. Seuss poem out of this mishnah: "I will build it on a boat, I will build it on a goat, I will build it in a tree, I will build it by the sea...." What modern places could you think of to add to this list of where a *sukkah* might be creatively placed?

3. Queen Helena is an important figure in rabbinic literature. She converted to Judaism and was one of its most pious practitioners. Evidently, she had quite a lavish sukkah; perhaps so large that it contained rooms so she was able to invite many visitors at once. We invite "*ushpizin*", spiritual guests, into our sukkah each year. Who would you invite in addition to the traditional seven (Abraham, Isaac, Jacob, Joseph, Moses, Aaron and David)? Will you make Helena part of your Sukkot celebration?

Shemini Atzeret

CHARITY

Deuteronomy 15:7-8

If there be among you a needy man, one of your brethren, within any of your gates, in your land which the Lord your God gives you, you shall not harden your heart, nor shut your hand from your needy brother, but you shall surely open your hand unto him and shall surely lend him sufficient funds for his need in that which he wants.

Mishnah Peah 8:9

Anyone who does not need public charity and takes it will become dependent on others before he dies. And anyone who is in need of charity and does not take it, will support others from his own money before he dies of old age.

Bavli Baba Metzia 31b

"You shall surely open" (Deuteronomy 15:11). Here we learn that you must give to the poor of your own city. From where do I know that you must give to the poor of another city? The verse teaches "Pato'ach tiftach" (the verb for "open" is doubled)–meaning, in all cases.

Discussion Questions

1. Why do you think the Torah tells us not to harden our hearts before telling us not to shut our hands? What connection is there between Pharoah's hardened heart (*l'chabed lev*) and this hard heart (*l'ametz lev*)?

2. This mishnah gives us an example of "Jewish karma": What goes around comes around. Can you think of examples of this phenomenon in other Jewish sources? In your own life?

3. Far or near, large or small, the Gemara tells us we must give *tzedakah*. (The sages deduce this by a playful interpretation of the emphatic Hebrew double verb form. The sages make each part of the verb apply to a different situation.) What are some ways you can incorporate this idea of charity into your own life? Are there other ways to interpret this doubled form of the verb in our Torah text?

How could you double the amount of generosity in your life?

Simchat Torah

ENDINGS AND BEGINNINGS

Deuteronomy 34:10-12

And no prophet has ever arisen like Moses, who knew God face to face. God sent him to do all the signs and wonders in the land of Egypt to Pharaoh and his servants and all his land and everything was done with a strong hand and all the great wonders that Moses did were before Israel.

Genesis 1:1-5

In a beginning God created the heavens and the earth. The earth was dark and disorganized and dimness was on the face of the deep and God's spirit hovered over the face of the waters. And God said, "Let there be light." And there was light. And God saw that the light was good and God made a difference between the light and the darkness. And God called the light "Day," and called the dark "Night," and there was evening and there was morning, the first day. (Genesis 1:1-5)

Mishnah Taanit 4:3

On the first day of the week they would read the first verses from the Torah from "in a beginning" (Genesis 1:1), to "and let there be a dome in the heavens" (Genesis 1:5). On the second day they would read from "and let there be a dome in the heavens" (Genesis 1:5), to "and let the waters be gathered together" (Genesis 1:6-8).

Bavli Rosh Hashanah 21b

Fifty gates of understanding were created in the world and all were given to Moses except one.

Discussion Questions

1. These two passages conclude, and begin, the Torah. What are their similarities and their differences?

2. In ancient Israel, while the Temple stood, regional representatives would go to Jerusalem to serve in the Temple. During that time, their communities at home would read the first chapter of Genesis. How did the Temple rites continue the work of creation? Does it make sense that the sages saw Jerusalem as the belly button of the world?

3. The cycle of reading Torah brings us ever-increasing levels of understanding. This insight from the Babylonian Talmud suggests that, no matter how far we progress, we always have further to go. (If Moses did not reach the final pinnacle of understanding, how can we expect that we shall?) How many levels of understanding have you experienced thus far?

Pesach

See also Bo, p.30

When we read the Haggadah, we are reading selections from the Torah, Mishnah, and the Gemara! Look for Biblical verses throughout. You will find evidence of the Mishnah in the Four Questions and the three symbols of Pesach. The Gemara is present in the rest of the seder.

End of Pesach

MIRIAM THE SONGSTRESS

Exodus:20-21

And Miriam the prophetess, Aaron's sister, took a tambourine in her hand and all the women followed her with instruments and dances. And Miriam led them in song: "Sing to God who is incredibly great. Both Egyptians horses and chariots has God thrown into the sea."

Mishnah Moed Katan 3:8-9

When a funeral is held during the middle days of Passover and Sukkot, women may wail for the dead but they do not clap their hands. But Rabbi Yishmael says: those who are close to the corpse may clap their hands....

What is a wail? When all the women sing together.

What is a dirge? When one woman sings and the rest answer after her.

Bavli Moed Katan 28a

Why is the story of Miriam's death (Numbers 20:1) placed next to the chapter concerning the red heifer (Numbers 19)? It is there to tell you that just as the red heifer atones for sin, so does the death of the righteous atone for sin.

Discussion Questions

1.Miriam was clearly a leader of prayer and, even more, a prophetess. How do you imagine her in her role as a prophet? How would she be like Moses? How would she be different? Why does the text emphasize that she is Aaron's sister and not Moses'?

2. The roots of the "call and response" genre of prayer are apparently quite ancient. Could we introduce more of this kind of musical prayer into our worship today?

3. Miriam held such an important position among the Israelites that when she had to stay outside the camp for seven days the entire nation stopped and waited for her (Numbers 12:15). What other women leaders can you think of in Jewish history who were this central to Judaism's survival and growth?

Shavuot

BIKKURIM
(see also Ki Tavo, p.100)

Deuteronomy 26:10-11

"Now, behold! I have brought the first fruits of the earth which God has
given to me." And with that he shall lay his basket of first fruits down
before the Lord your God and bow before the Lord your God. And
you shall be happy with all the goodness which the Lord your God has
given to you and your family, to the Levites and to the non-Jews who live
among you.

Mishnah Bikkurim 3:9

They decorated the basket of first fruits on the outside with the seven
species that the Torah mentions growing in Israel (i.e., grapes, figs, olives,
pomegranates, dates, barley and wheat).

Sifre Deuteronomy Piska 301

When one goes into his field and sees a ripe fig, a ripe cluster of grapes, or
a ripe pomegranate, he should tie them with strings and say, "These shall
be my first fruits."

Discussion Questions

1. The text here commands us to be happy. Can anyone command someone else to feel a certain emotion? How can you help yourself to feel happy?

2. Below is an illustration of part of a 1500-year-old mosaic synagogue floor in Sephhoris in Israel. It shows the basket of the first fruits with the seven species on top and two pigeons on either side. The plates chained together are cymbals that would have been used in the march to Jerusalem. Shavuot was an elaborate county fair/parade. How could we make our observance of Shavuot more joyous and rich with traditions?

3. This passage from the midrash describes how one would identify the actual first fruit. What are your first fruits today? How can you show God your appreciation for them?

The Major Documents of Rabbinic Literature

Rabbinic literature is made up of five major works, each of which has its own characteristic traits. Because all five sources of material appear in this volume, a brief introduction is in order.

The five main works are the Mishnah, the Tosefta, the Talmud of the Land of Israel (the Yerushalmi), the Midrash collections, and the Talmud of Babylonia (the Bavli). Those parts of the Talmuds which are commentary on the Mishnah are called Gemara. The term "Talmud" refers to the Mishnah and Gemara combined.

	Date Finished	Place Finished
Mishnah	200 C.E.	The Land of Israel
Tosefta	220-230 C.E.	The Land of Israel
Yerushalmi	400 C.E.	The Land of Israel
Midrash	400-500 C.E.	The Land of Israel
Bavli	427-520 C.E.	Babylonia

The foundation document of rabbinic literature is the Mishnah. Its component parts, called *mishnayot*, were composed after the destruction of the Temple in 70 C.E. These *mishnayot*, oral teachings, were promulgated in many schools and were finally culled, organized and codified by Rabbi Yehudah HaNasi around 200 C.E.

Instead of being organized according to the structure of the Torah, the Mishnah is organized according to six overarching topics: Seeds, Seasons, Civil Law, Women, Holy Things, and Purities. In all six of these orders, the format of the Mishnah remains constant. Its language is formulated for easy memorization. The Mishnah outlines the sages' vision of how they wanted the world to be, and transmits very little of how the world actually was. In some cases, its teachings are completely theoretical—exercises in logic, rather than law meant to be applied to everyday life.

Tosefta means "additions," and as its name indicates, it contains additional viewpoints and commentary on subjects found in the Mishnah. The Tosefta is approximately four times larger than the Mishnah. It is generally agreed that it was composed in the Land of Israel, one generation after the redaction of the Mishnah, i.e., 220-230 C.E. Tosefta provides commentary to all six orders of the Mishnah.

The next group of texts to be organized and published were the tana'itic midrashim, which show how the law of the Mishna-era rabbis (known at *tana'im*) can be drawn out from closely analyzing the Torah (the process known as *midrash*). Following the flow of the biblical texts (rather than the Mishnah's topical arrangement), these works are *Mekhilta d'Rabbi Yishmael* (on Exodus), *Sifra* (on Leviticus), and *Sifre* (on Numbers and om Deuteronomy), and were probably completed around 300 C.E.

Mekhilta de-Rabbi Yishmael contains some of the oldest material found in the midrash collections, but it is difficult to say when it was finished. *Sifre* on Deuteronomy is most often thought to be a midrash compilation from this same era, but it is not a homogeneous work and different component sections of this work originated in different periods and circles. *Sifra*, the commentary on the book of Leviticus, and *Sifre* on Numbers, like the other tana'itic midrashim, probably date from the second half of the third century and underwent further development.

The other, and later, group of midrashic texts are called the aggadic midrashim. *"Aggadah"* is from the Hebrew word for tale. These volumes feature the sort of fanciful tales which have made midrash a popular genre for more than a thousand years. Rather than drawing verse-by-verse connections between the Torah and rabbinic teachings, these texts– *Genesis Rabbah, Leviticus Rabbah, Lamentations Rabbah, Pesikta d'Rav Kahana,* and *Tanhuma*–compile sermons and other rabbinic teachings on the biblical books.

Genesis Rabbah, the exposition of the first book of the Torah, came to closure in the Land of Israel in the fifth century (probably in its first half), a troubled time and place in Jewish history.

Rome had accepted Christianity with Constantine's conversion in 312 C.E. At this stage, Judaism was a protected religion: Jews could not be forced to violate the Sabbath. Then, in 360 C.E., Julian (Christians call him "the apostate") reaffirmed paganism and threw off Christianity. As part of his program to embarrass the Christians, in 368 C.E., he gave the Jews permission to rebuild the Temple, thereby disproving Jesus' prediction that no stone on stone of the Temple would remain. However, Julian died within the year, and the Jews' hopes for rebuilding the Temple were dashed. Now Judaism became a persecuted religion. Israel's rights to security and freedom were limited. Synagogues were destroyed, and Jews lost the right to convert slaves they had purchased. In contrast, Jews who became Christians enjoyed the protection of the state. By the turn of the fifth century, around 410, Jews' institution of self-government in the land of Israel came to an end. In sum, it was a very difficult time.

The teachings of the midrash collections *Genesis Rabbah* and *Leviticus Rabbah*, which reached closure about 400-500 C.E., helped Jews deal with the new realities of Roman rule and the absence of the Temple.

The Talmud of the Land of Israel, called the Yerushalmi, appears to have been redacted in the early fifth century. One of the Yerushalmi's most distinctive features is its paucity of midrashic material, i.e., stories and biblical exegesis, when compared with the Babylonian Talmud (the Bavli). Approximately one-sixth of the Yerushalmi's bulk is aggadah (stories), while in the Bavli the proportion is almost a third. Another characteristic of the Yerushalmi is the relatively less rigorous and elaborate editing process it underwent (when compared with the Bavli).

The commentary to the Mishnah, i.e., the Gemara, of the Babylonian Talmud, also known as the Bavli, was completed as early as 427-520, or as late as the mid-seventh century.

The Bavli has a character all its own. Like the Yerushalmi, it is a commentary to the Mishnah. It uses all the sources previously composed by the sages in its commentary, including: Tosefta, tana'itic teachings not included in the Mishnah (*baraitot*), passages from the Yerushalmi and the midrash collections. The Bavli also adds its own materials to the mix; stories and sayings of the sages, as well as detailed analysis of earlier materials, called stammaitic material. When you feel yourself wanting to use your thumb and say, "on the *one* hand...on the *other* hand," you're almost certainly in stammaitic material.

An Anthromorphic Portrait
of Rabbinic Texts

How do these five different kinds of Rabbinic literature differ one from another? In general, the Mishnah, which was compiled first, is more theoretical than practical. Practical details are provided by the Tosefta, Midrash, Yerushalmi and the Bavli.

One way to understand the interrelationship of these Rabbinic writings is to think about them as different personality types. Mishnah is a dreamer, who's always imagining how things should be rather than thinking about how they are. This sort of person is always concocting beautiful schemes to organize her life. The only problem is that these dreams don't necessarily relate to reality.

Tosefta is the Mishnah's more practical friend. When the Mishnah goes off on an idealistic tangent, Tosefta says, "Wait a minute. I don't think that's going to work. And what if conditions change? Have you thought of all the consequences?"

The Yerushalmi resembles Tosefta, only more so. The Yerushalmi listens to the Mishnah and Tosefta and then takes over the conversation, citing statistics and information from a vast library of knowledge. The Yerushalmi may take a long time to come to a decision, but usually it will eventually tell you that, "Yes, the Mishnah's plan will work," or "No, the Mishnah's plan won't work, but Tosefta's might," or "Neither the Mishnah nor the Tosefta have it right. However, I've dug up an answer which I think *will* work."

The Midrash collections, which comment on different books of the Bible rather than on the Mishnah (in contrast to the rest of Rabbinic literature), are loners. They're loosely connected to the Mishnah, Tosefta, Yerushalmi, and Bavli, but they really go their own way. Midrash is that one member of a circle of friends who is included, but not terribly attached. And is that one into telling stories!

Finally, the Bavli is like the Yerushalmi...and not like the Yerushalmi. Like the Yerushalmi, the Bavli listens to the Mishnah and Tosefta and then takes over the conversation. However, unlike the Yerushalmi, the Bavli isn't so "bottom line" oriented. The Bavli is more interested in exploring options than in determining the one right solution to a problem. Also, the Bavli loves to tell stories; almost as much as Midrash does. Finally, the Bavli is a bit more talkative than the Yerushalmi–who was already quite talkative.

If you ever gathered these five "people" in a room, the Mishnah would start the conversation, next Tosefta would get in a few comments, then the conversation would be taken over by the Yerushalmi (let's say, someone from Israel) and the Bavli (let's say, someone from New York City). Midrash would be over in a corner studying Torah and occasionally contributing to the conversation.

About the Author

Judith Z. Abrams was ordained at Hebrew Union College in 1985. She earned her Ph.D. in Rabbinic literature from the Baltimore Hebrew University in 1993.

Rabbi Abrams is the founder and director of Maqom: A School for Adult Talmud Study, online, (http://www.maqom.com), where everyone, regardless of their background, can learn.

She received the Covenant Award for outstanding performance in the field of Jewish Education. She teaches through the Siegal College Distance Learning Program and the ALEPH rabbinic program and is the author of many books about Talmud and prayer.

Rabbi Abrams is available to speak and teach throughout the country, as she has done for many years .

She can be reached at Maqom, POB 3190--323, Houston, TX 77231, (713) 723-2918, email: maqom@compassnet.com.

Other Books by Rabbi Abrams

The Babylonian Talmud: A Topical Guide, 2002
Illness and Health in the Jewish Tradition: Writings from the Bible to Today, with David Freeman, M.D., 1999
A Beginner's Guide to the Steinsaltz Talmud, 1999
Judaism and Disability: Portrayals in Ancient Texts from the Tanach through the Bavli, 1998
Talmud for Beginners: Volume III, Living in a Non-Jewish World, 1997
The Women of the Talmud, 1995
Learn Talmud: How to Use the Steinsaltz English Talmud, 1995
Jewish Parenting: Rabbinic Insights. With Steven Abrams, 1994
The Talmud for Beginners: Volume II, Text, 1993
The Talmud for Beginners: Volume I, Prayer, 1991

Juvenile Titles

Gates of Repentance for Young People, 2002
Simchat Torah: A Family Celebration, 1995
A Family Sukkot Seder, 1993
Shabbat: A Family Service, 1991
Rosh Hashanah: A Family Service, 1990
Selichot: A Family Service, 1990
Yom Kippur: A Family Service, 1990

Colophon

This book was written on an Apple Macintosh G4 in Microsoft Word and was edited in OpenOffice 2 beta for Windows. Layout was designed in InDesign CS2. Cover photo was taken with a Canon PowerShot A520 and massaged in PhotoShop CS2. Text font is Adobe Garamond Premiere Pro.

Fern Weis gave invaluable advice as a first reader. The cheerful participation and feedback of Yael and Ariella Grossman is gratefully acknowledged. The genesis of this book goes back to 1995 and the Jewish Communications Network, so a special tip of the publisher's cap to visionary founding editor, Yori Yanover, and to the bold owners: Adi Ben-Jakob and Niv Bleich.

People who read the fine print at the back of books are likely to notice typographical and other errors elsewhere in the text. You know who you are. Let us know, too. Future editions will acknowledge by name everyone who lets us know about a previously unnoticed error at corrections@BenYehudaPress.com